KU-339-691

Longman Test Practice Kits

Science

Key Stage 3

Emily Sadler • *John Sadler*

Longman

Series editors
Geoff Black and Stuart Wall

Titles available
Key Stage 2
English
Mathematics
Science

Key Stage 3
English
Mathematics
Science

Addison Wesley Longman Ltd.,
Edinburgh Gate, Harlow,
CM20 2JE, England
and Associated Companies throughout the World

©Addison Wesley Longman 1998

All rights reserved; no part of this publication may be reproduced,
stored in a retrieval system, or transmitted in any form or by any means,
electronic, mechanical, photocopying, recording or otherwise without
either the prior written consent of the Publishers or a licence permitting
restricted copying in the United Kingdom issued by the Copyright
Licensing Agency Ltd, 90 Tottenham Court Road, London, W1P 9HE.

First Published 1998

ISBN 0582 31571-9

British Library Cataloguing-in-Publication Data
A catalogue record for this book is available from the British Library.

Set by 30 in 10.5/16 pt Frutiger

Produced by Longman Singapore Publishers Pte, Ltd.
Printed in Singapore

Table of contents

Acknowledgements

We are grateful for the work of the staff at Addison Wesley Longman, in particular Bridget Allen for her helpful comments and suggestions. We would also like to thank Stuart Wall for the many enjoyable meetings we had over tea and cakes in Cambridge which helped us to formulate our ideas. Finally, we must thank our partners Alison and Paul for their patience and encouragement during the preparation of this book.

The National Tests

How they work

- During years 7 to 9 your child will be studying Science, Mathematics and English as part of Key Stage 3 of the National Curriculum. At the end of year 9 (at age 14) your child will take National Tests in each of these subjects.
- These written National Tests (sometimes called SATs) will take place in May of year 9. Your child takes these tests in their own school, but they will be marked by teachers from outside the school.
- There are two examination papers for Science, each lasting 1 hour.
- You will receive the results of your child's National Tests by the end of July. You will also receive the result of assessments made by your child's teachers in the classroom.
- Your child's results will be expressed as a *Level* for both The National Tests and for the assessment by their teachers.
- You will also receive a summary of the Key Stage 3 results received by all the other pupils in your child's school, and for all pupils nationally. You will then be able to check your child's progress against other pupils of their age.

Levels of achievement

Achievement in each subject is divided into Levels 1 to 8 at Key Stage 3. Level 8 is the highest Level and Level 1 the lowest. You can see from the diagram below that your child is expected to reach Level 5 or 6 by the end of Key Stage 3 (the end of year 9).

☐ Exceptional performance	Above level 8	☐	Level 4 ▨
	Level 8	▨	Level 3 ▨
☐ Exceeded target for age group	Level 7	▨	Level 2 ▨
	Level 6	▨	Level 1 ▨
▨ Achieved target for age group	Level 5	▨	
▨ Working toward target for age group			

Levels of entry (tiers)

- There are two tiers for the National Test Papers for Science.
- Your child will usually be entered either for Test Papers covering Levels 3–6 or Levels 5–7. Your child's teachers will decide which tier they should be entered for. This is to make sure that your child is taking a paper that he or she can do.
- In this book we are concentrating on Levels 5–7.

Using this book

Science at Key Stage 3

In order to assess Science, the National Curriculum divides Science into four sections, called Attainment Targets (ATs).

AT1 Experimental and Investigative Science (teacher-assessed)
AT2 Life Processes and Living Things (mainly Biology)
AT3 Materials and their Properties (mainly Chemistry)
AT4 Physical Processes (mainly Physics)

AT2, AT3 and AT4 are examined in the National Tests. On page 3 is a list of all the topics your child has to know about for each of these Attainment Targets. Your child's teacher will assess AT1.

Part 1 Self-check revision

Part 1 (pages 3–38) gives you a brief outline of the topics that your child needs to revise for the National Test for Science. Please work through Part1 *before* trying the actual tests in Part 2.

We have tried to make using this book more interesting by asking your child to fill in blanks in the text and on the diagrams. This exercise will help your child to check their understanding of the topic. Answers to all the blank spaces can be found at the end of Part 1 (page 38).

On page 3 there is a progress chart; tick the topic when your child has revised and understood the topic completely. For more information on a topic use the *Longman Homework Handbook Key Stage 3 Science* or the *Longman GCSE Study Guide Science*.

Part 2 Test practice papers

Part 2 contains the following:

- **Words of command** Explanation of words used in your Science Test Papers.
- **Questions** Two full test practice papers for Levels 5–7.
- **Answers and mark scheme** Full solutions and marking for all the questions, with a reference guide to Part 1. As parent, you should take responsibility for making the Tests.
- **Examiner tips** Helpful advice from an examiner to help you to improve your child's score.
- **Level chart** A guide to the marks needed to achieve each Level.

The questions will assess your child's ability in the following skills:

- knowledge and understanding
- handling information
- interpretation and evaluation
- problem solving.

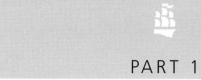

PART 1

Self-check revision

In this part of the book you will find a brief, easy-to-use review of the key facts you are expected to know for your National Test. These cover the 13 topic areas identified in the National Curriculum for Science and outlined in the 'Programme of Study'.

To help make your revision more active and interesting, you will find 10 blank spaces to fill in for each of the 13 topic areas. Answers can be found at the end of Part 1 (page 38).

After you have revised a topic, and completed the blanks in that topic, place a tick in the appropriate space in the following progress chart. This will help you to keep a record of your progress. It will be best if you revise all the topics *before* you attempt the test practice papers in Part 2 of the book.

Revision progress chart

	Topic	Tick when revised
1	**Life processes and cell activity**	
2	**Humans as organisms**	
2.1	Nutrition	
2.2	Circulation	
2.3	Movement	
2.4	Reproduction	
2.5	Breathing	
2.6	Health	
3	**Green plants as organisms**	
3.1	Nutrition and growth	
3.2	Reproduction	
3.3	Respiration	
4	**Variation, classification and inheritance**	
4.1	Variation	
4.2	Classification	
4.3	Inheritance	
5	**Living things in their environment**	
5.1	Adaptation	
5.2	Feeding relationships	
5.3	Competition	

BIOLOGY

	Topic	Tick when revised
6	**Classifying materials**	
6.1	Solids, liquids and gases	
6.2	Elements	
6.3	Compounds	
6.4	Mixtures	
6.5	Metals and non-metals	
7	**Changing materials**	
7.1	Physical changes	
7.2	Geological changes	
7.3	Chemical reactions	
8	**Patterns of behaviour**	
8.1	Metals	
8.2	Acids and bases	
9	**Electricity and magnetism**	
9.1	Static charge	
9.2	Current in circuits	
9.3	Magnetic fields	
9.4	Electromagnets	
10	**Forces and motion**	
10.1	Force and linear motion	
10.2	Force and rotation	
10.3	Force and pressure	
11	**Light and sound**	
11.1	The behaviour of light	
11.2	Hearing	
11.3	Vibration and sound	
12	**The Earth and beyond**	
13	**Energy resources and energy transfer**	
13.1	Energy resources	
13.2	Conservation of energy	

CHEMISTRY

PHYSICS

Life processes and cell activity

Organs are made up of lots of cells. There are many different organs in animals and plants. Each organ does a special job.

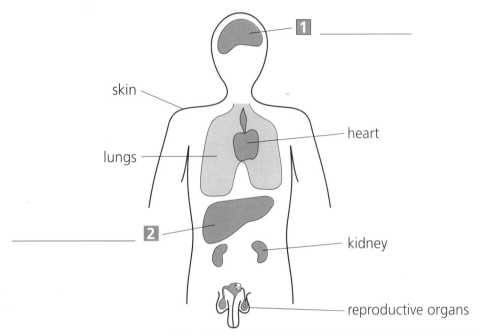

Animal organ	Job
lungs	swap carbon dioxide (waste gas) for oxygen
3 _____	controls the amount of water in the body and gets rid of waste
brain	is the control centre of the body
4 _____	pumps blood around the body
liver	controls the amount of blood sugar and minerals
skin	is a protective layer that keeps things out (and in!)
reproductive organs	allow humans to reproduce (have babies)

In plants the main organs are the flowers, leaves, roots, stems and seeds.

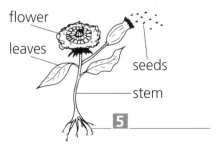

Answers can be found on page 38

5

Plant organ	Job
flower	contains the male and female reproductive parts
leaves	make food by photosynthesis
6 _____	moves water and minerals up and down the plant
roots	hold the plant in the soil and get water and minerals out of the soil
seeds	are spread and develop into a new plant

Animals and plants are made up of a wide variety of cells. Cells make up tissue. Tissue makes 7 _____. Organs make systems.

A typical animal cell is *not* the same as a typical plant cell.

A typical animal cell   *A typical plant cell*

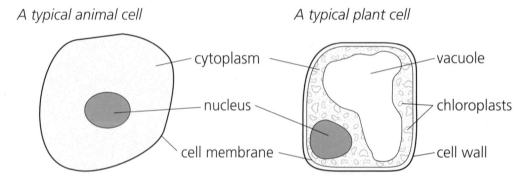

Part of plant cell	Job
nucleus	contains the chromosomes and controls the cell
cytoplasm	transfers energy, makes things and stores food
cell membrane	controls the movement of substances into and out of the cell
8 _____	contain chlorophyll which gives the plant its green colour
vacuole	stores useful substances and water
9 _____	is a strong layer that makes the cell strong

Some cells are very special. They have become special shapes so they can do very special jobs. We say these cells have **adapted** for a purpose. Ciliated epithelial cells, sperm, ova, palisade cells and root hair cells are all examples of specialized cells.

Answers can be found on page 38

Cell name	Diagram	Job
ciliated epithelial cell	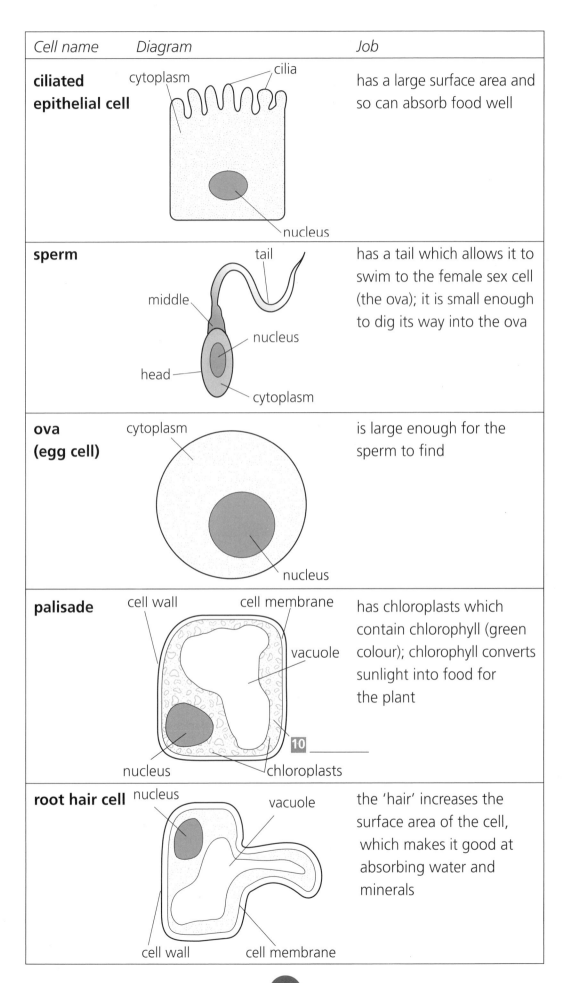	has a large surface area and so can absorb food well
sperm		has a tail which allows it to swim to the female sex cell (the ova); it is small enough to dig its way into the ova
ova (egg cell)		is large enough for the sperm to find
palisade		has chloroplasts which contain chlorophyll (green colour); chlorophyll converts sunlight into food for the plant
root hair cell		the 'hair' increases the surface area of the cell, which makes it good at absorbing water and minerals

topic **2**

Humans as organisms

2.1 Nutrition

Humans need to eat a balanced diet to stay healthy. A balanced diet contains carbohydrates, fats, fibre, minerals, **1**_____ , vitamins and water. We can have a balanced diet by eating a variety of foods.

Nutrient	How it helps keep the body healthy	Foods that contain the nutrient
carbohydrates	provide energy	bread, potatoes
2_____	store energy	butter, margarine
fibre	provides bulk	cereals, bread
minerals	small amounts needed for specific purposes, e.g. iron for our blood	fruit, milk, cheese, green vegetables, meat
proteins	building and repairing	cheese, fish, meat, milk, beans
vitamins	small amounts needed for specific purposes, e.g. vitamin C for healthy teeth and skin	fruit, vegetables, dairy products, fish oil, liver
water	for healthy blood and cells	fruit, vegetables

We use food to allow us to grow and repair ourselves, and as a fuel (source of energy) so we can be active. When we are more active we need more energy. The best fuels comes from foods that contain carbohydrates (e.g. sugar and starch). The body combines carbohydrates with oxygen (from the air we breathe) and turns them into carbon dioxide (which we breathe out), water and energy. This process is called **respiration**.

Answers can be found on page 38

Digestion is the process by which food is broken down so that it can be absorbed. Food is chewed to break it down into smaller pieces that can be easily swallowed.

The small pieces are broken down further by the action of acids and **3**_____. This process occurs in stages as food passes through the gut.

Eventually, food molecules pass through the lining of the small intestine into the blood stream. Water is also absorbed. Anything left in the intestine, mainly cellulose, cannot be digested and is waste material.

Waste material is passed out of the **4**_____ by a process known as **egestion**.

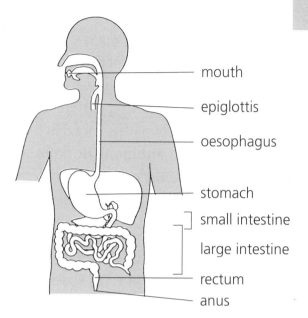

mouth

epiglottis

oesophagus

stomach

small intestine

large intestine

rectum

anus

2.2 Circulation

Blood travels all round the body. It is used to take and remove materials to and from different parts of the body. Blood flows through blood vessels. There are three types of blood vessel: arteries, veins and capillaries.

Blood vessel	Description
arteries	thick, muscular vessels that carry blood away from the heart
5_____	thinner, less muscular vessels that carry blood to the heart
capillaries	thin, narrow blood vessels that join arteries and veins together; nutrients and waste materials are exchanged between the blood and the organs

2.3 Movement

Bones connected by joints, surrounded by and joined to muscles, make up our **6**_____. The skeleton gives the body its general shape and provides a protective cage for our organs. It also has some very strong bones which support our weight and help to keep us upright.

Answers can be found on page 38

When certain bones meet, such as at the elbow or knee, a joint is formed that allows the skeleton to move. Movement of joints is controlled by muscles. Muscles can only contract (pull). For this reason they are always found in pairs called **antagonistic pairs**. When one muscle contracts the other muscle is forced to relax.

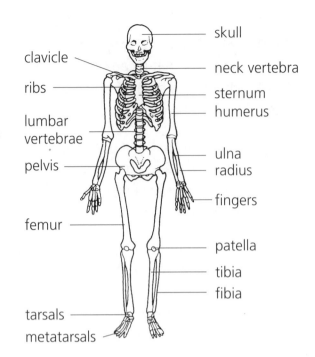

The arm bends and straightens using the bicep and tricep muscles. When the bicep muscle contracts the arm bends. When the tricep muscle contracts the arm straightens. The tricep and bicep work together but in opposite directions. They are an example of an antagonistic pair of muscles.

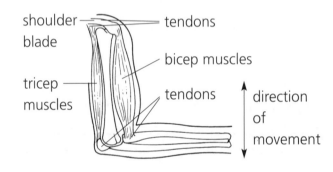

2.4 Reproduction

Adolescence or puberty is the time when children change into adults. Some of the physical and emotional changes that take place during puberty are shown in the table.

Boys only	Boys and girls	Girls only
penis gets larger	grow taller	menstruation starts
voice deepens	pubic hair grows	breasts develop
facial hair grows	mood swings	hips get wider
become more muscular	sexual dreams	additional fat on thighs

Males and females have different reproductive organs. Males make sperm in their **7**_____ constantly from the start of adolescence until death. Females have **8**_____ which are full of ova (eggs) at birth, but none are released until adolescence.

Answers can be found on page 38

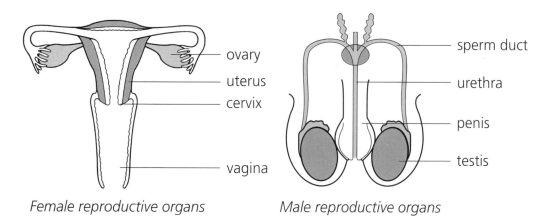

Female reproductive organs   *Male reproductive organs*

Approximately every 4 weeks an egg (ovum) is released from one of the two ovaries. The ovum moves down the fallopian tube (oviduct) and into the uterus (womb). The blood-rich lining of the uterus thickens during the time between the ovum being released and it reaching the uterus. If the ovum has not been fertilized by sperm, the ovum and lining will pass out of the body of the female through her vagina. This passing of blood is commonly called a 'period'. As soon as the bleeding stops another ovum is being prepared for its release from the ovaries and the cycle starts again.

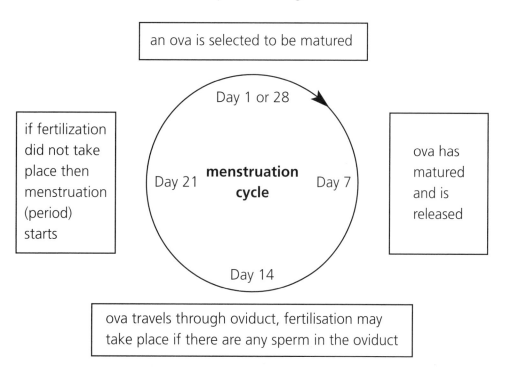

2.5 Breathing

When we breathe, air is taken into our lungs and stale air is removed. Lungs have a very large surface area made up of bronchioles and air sacs. The air sacs are very close to the capillaries, which allows for the exchange of oxygen and carbon dioxide.

Answers can be found on page 38

Small particles or certain chemicals in smoke and other fumes can damage the structure of the lungs. Smoking increases the chances of a person having diseases such as bronchitis, emphysema and lung cancer.

Aerobic respiration means that 9 _____ is needed for respiration. Oxygen reacts with glucose to form carbon dioxide and water. A large amount of energy is given off during this process. The reaction is very similar to glucose burning in oxygen:

glucose + oxygen ⟶ carbon dioxide + water + energy

2.6 Health

Drugs, when prescribed by doctors, can be very helpful to ill people.

Drug	Example	Effect
sedative (depressants)	alcohol; sleeping pills; tranquillizers	slows down brain; makes you sleepy
pain killer (analgesic)	aspirin; paracetamol; morphine	reduces sense of pain
stimulant	caffeine; amphetamines; cocaine; nicotine	speeds up brain; makes you feel more alert
antibiotic	penicillin	kills or inactivates germs

Most human diseases are caused by bacteria and viruses. Once these enter our bodies they reproduce rapidly; this is called the incubation period. After a period of time we begin to feel unwell and start to show the symptoms of the illness. Most of us produce antibodies that attack the germs and try to kill them.

Immunization is a way of protecting us against getting diseases. Some dead germs (vaccine) are put into the blood stream. The vaccine causes antibodies to be formed, ready to fight the disease in case we come into contact with that disease. You may have been vaccinated during your lifetime to stop you catching measles, tuberculosis (TB), rubella, diptheria, whooping cough and polio.

We are also given medicines to help us get better. You have probably taken an **antibiotic** at some time in your life. Antibiotics either kill germs or stop them from having any effect. Unfortunately, antibiotics do not work against viruses.

Remember 10 _____, *NOT prescribed to you by your doctor can seriously damage your health.*

Answers can be found on page 38

Green plants as organisms

3.1 Nutrition and growth

Green plants convert carbon dioxide and water into carbohydrates and oxygen by a process called

1 _____ .

Carbohydrates contain carbon, hydrogen and oxygen. Carbohydrates are an example of **biomass** (biological mass). For photosynthesis to take place sunlight and chlorophyll are needed. Chlorophyll is the catalyst for the reaction:

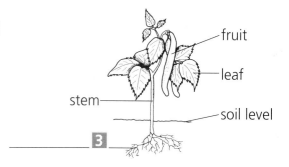

carbon dioxide + water ⟶ carbohydrates + **2** _____ .
Energy is taken in from the sunlight.

Nitrogen and other elements, as well as carbon, hydrogen and oxygen, are needed for plant growth.

Root hairs absorb water and various minerals into the plant from the soil.

3.2 Reproduction

The flowers of a plant contain reproductive organs. **Pollination** takes place when pollen is carried from the male part of a flower (anther), to the female part of a flower (stigma).

Fertilization takes place when pollen enters the **6** _____ .
The ovules eventually become the seeds of the plant. The ovary becomes the **7** _____ .

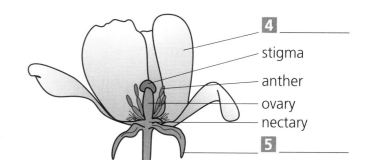

3.3 Respiration

During the night plants need oxygen to break down carbohydrates into carbon dioxide and **8** _____ .

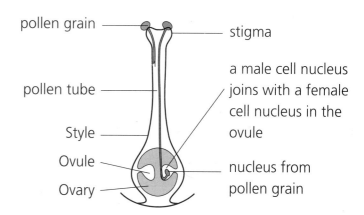

During this process energy is released. This type of respiration is known as **9** _____ respiration.

carbohydrates + oxygen ⟶ **10** _____ + water + energy

Answers can be found on page 38

Variation, classification and inheritance

4.1 Variation

There is a large amount of variation both within species and between species. For example, people belonging to the same family are not identical. Brothers and sisters do not look the same. There are two types of variation: **continuous variation** (such as height) and **1**_____ **variation** (such as inherited diseases). Some people are tall, some people are short and others are in between – there is a continuous variation. But with inherited diseases, such as cystic fibrosis, you either have the disease or you don't – it is discontinuous.

Experiments on identical twins show that variation can be brought about by both inheritance and the **2**_____. Identical twins that were brought up together are compared with identical twins that have been brought up separately. Identical twins have the same **3**_____. Any differences must be due to their environment, such as their diet, their school, their home; any similarities must be due to inheritance.

4.2 Classification

Keys can be used to identify animals and plants. A key is a series of questions you have to answer to identify a plant or animal. Each question has a 'yes' or 'no' answer. The key can either be in the form of a diagram (a tree key) or a series of questions (a number tree).

This is a **tree key** that tells you if a plant was a daffodil, a daisy or a poppy. You should be able to design a different key to identify each of these three flowers.

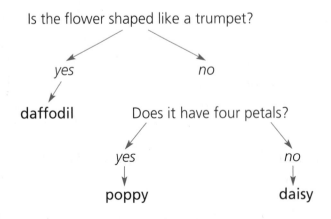

Answers can be found on page 38

14

This is a **number key** that tells you if an animal is a robin, a snail or a squirrel.

1 Does it have a backbone?   yes – go to **2**

                                   no – it is a **4** _____

2 Does it have feathers?   yes – it is a **5** _____

                                   no – it is a **6** _____

You should be able to think of another key to identify these three animals.

Living things can be classified into **7** _____ or **kingdoms**. The two main groups are plants and **8** _____. Nowadays classification is based on the five kingdom system: plants, fungi, animals, protista (e.g. sponges) and monera (e.g. blue-green algae).

The animal kingdom can be further grouped into animals with backbones (**vertebrates**) and animals without backbones (**9** _____).

These can be further broken down:

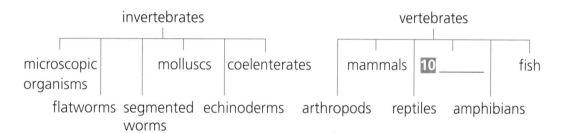

Similarly, the plant kingdom can be divided into further groups:

4.3 Inheritance

Selective breeding can lead to new varieties. You may know that a mule is a cross between a horse and a donkey. (Mules are sterile and cannot breed.) You may have been to dog shows or cat shows. The owners have bred these animals from the best parents available to them. Horse owners pay large sums of money to breed from horses that have shown that they can run very fast.

Selective breeding of plants also takes place. Nowadays it is possible to buy plants that are resistant to diseases.

Answers can be found on page 38

Living things in their environment

5.1 Adaptation

The place where an organism occurs is called its **1**_____ . Different habitats support different plants and animals. Examples of habitats are ponds, seashores, woods and deserts. The conditions that make up an organism's habitat are called the **2**_____ .

Organisms adapt to their environmental conditions, such as temperature, seasons, light intensity and humidity. Some birds migrate to warmer places in the winter; certain animals such as tortoises hibernate; certain plants die back and seeds remain dormant until the weather becomes warmer. Some animals such as cockroaches and earthworms turn away from light.

5.2 Feeding relationships

A **food chain** is a series of feeding relationships between organisms living in the same community. You are probably familiar with the following food chain:

lettuces ⟶ rabbits ⟶ foxes

Lettuces are eaten by rabbits which are eaten by foxes.

Rabbits are herbivores – they eat *only* **3**_____ . Foxes are carnivores – they eat *only* animals. Humans eat both plants and animals – they are called **4**_____ .

In any food chain, organisms can be put into one of three groups: producers, **5**_____ and decomposers. Plants can make their food from simple substances and sunlight. Because they make food they are called the **6**_____ . Animals that eat only plants are called the **primary consumers**. All herbivores are primary consumers. Many animals eat other animals – these are called **secondary consumers**. The animals that eat the secondary consumers are called **tertiary consumers**.

Decomposers are tiny creatures called bacteria that break down materials into simpler substances. They are not always shown in a food chain.

A **food web** shows what eats what in a whole community. In a food web there are several food chains because some animals feed on a large number of different things; and some animals, like humans, are omnivores.

Answers can be found on page 38

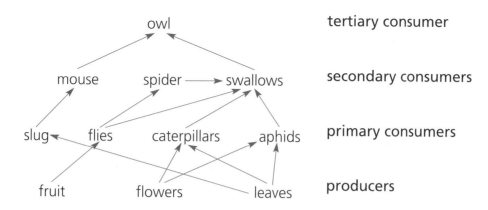

A **pyramid of numbers** shows the relative number of organisms at each feeding level. The width of each band indicates the number of organisms. The shape can vary depending upon the number of producers, the number of primary consumers and the number of secondary **7**_____ . One might look like this:

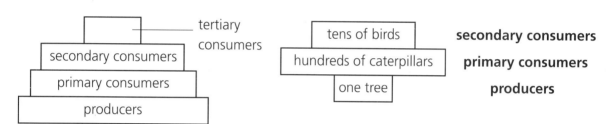

Sometimes poisonous materials get into the food chain. You may have read about DDT, which was used to kill mosquitoes. It was sprayed on lakes. DDT is not easily broken down and it was absorbed by plankton. The plankton was eaten by small fish, the small fish were eaten by larger fish, and the larger fish were eaten by birds. If you think about this chain, you will realise that the concentration of DDT in birds was very large and it made them die. Nowadays DDT is not used.

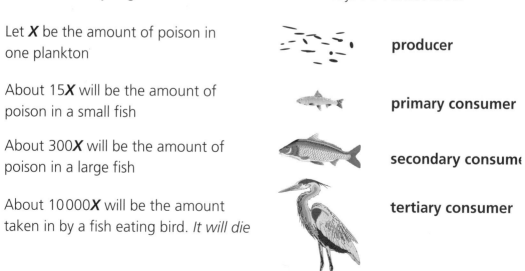

Let **X** be the amount of poison in one plankton — **producer**

About 15**X** will be the amount of poison in a small fish — **primary consumer**

About 300**X** will be the amount of poison in a large fish — **secondary consume**

About 10 000**X** will be the amount taken in by a fish eating bird. *It will die* — **tertiary consumer**

Answers can be found on page 38

5.3 Competition

Various factors affect the size of a population, such as **predation** and **competition** for resources. The predator eats another animal called the
8_____. Predators are carnivores; the prey can be a carnivore or a herbivore. If a predator has a very narrow range of prey that it likes, the population of each will have a strong effect on one another.

Population is affected by the availability of **9**_____. We know that rabbits breed very rapidly, but the number of rabbits cannot keep increasing because there will come a point when there are not enough plants to feed all the rabbits.

If an organism can successfully compete in its environment then it will produce many offspring for the next generation. These in turn will be successful because of their inherited adaptations. This process is known as
10_____.

Answers can be found on page 38

6 Classifying materials

topic

6.1 Solids, liquids and gases

	How dense? (high, medium or low)	Can it be compressed (squeezed)?	Will it flow?	Does it maintain its shape?	Does it maintain its volume?
solid	high	no	**1**_____	yes	yes
liquid	medium	no	yes	no	**2**_____
gas	low	**3**_____	yes	no	no

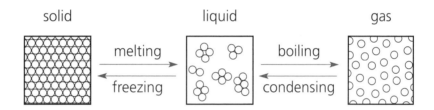

In a solid the particles are close together. When we heat a solid the particles move further apart, and eventually it will become a liquid. When we heat a liquid it will eventually boil and become a **4**_____.

If the pressure is increased the particles of a gas move closer together. This reduces the volume of the gas.

The movement of particles from one place to another is called **diffusion**.

6.2 Elements

Elements are made up of lots of atoms. All the atoms of the same element have the same number of protons.

Elements can be represented by chemical symbols.

Name of element	sodium	hydrogen	carbon	chlorine	oxygen	**6**_____
Symbol	Na	H	C	Cl	**5**__	K

Answers can be found on page 38

6.3 Compounds

When two or more elements combine in a chemical reaction a **compound** is formed. The name given to the compound usually tells us which elements made it.

Elements reacting	Compound formed
carbon (C) + oxygen (O_2)	carbon dioxide (CO_2)
magnesium (Mg) + oxygen (O_2)	magnesium oxide (MgO)
sodium (Na) + chlorine (Cl_2)	sodium chloride (NaCl)
hydrogen (H_2) + **7** _____	water (H_2O)

6.4 Mixtures

Mixtures contain different elements and/or different compounds which are not chemically combined. Air is a mixture of gases. Air contains oxygen, nitrogen, carbon dioxide and other gases. Brine is a mixture of sodium chloride and **8** _____ .

Mixtures can be separated by physical methods (i.e. methods which do not involve chemical reactions). Some separation methods are listed below.

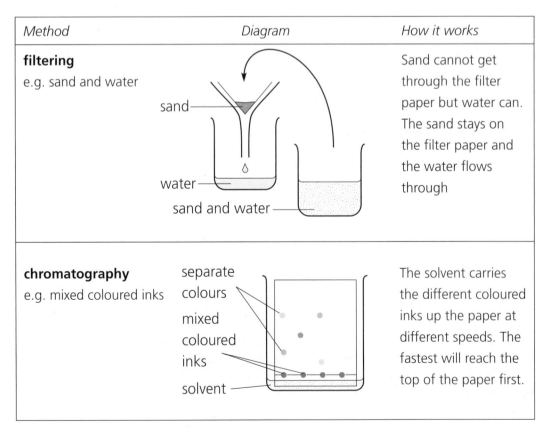

Method	Diagram	How it works
filtering e.g. sand and water	sand — water — sand and water —	Sand cannot get through the filter paper but water can. The sand stays on the filter paper and the water flows through
chromatography e.g. mixed coloured inks	separate colours — mixed coloured inks — solvent —	The solvent carries the different coloured inks up the paper at different speeds. The fastest will reach the top of the paper first.

Answers can be found on page 38

Method	Diagram	How it works
distillation e.g. ethanol and water	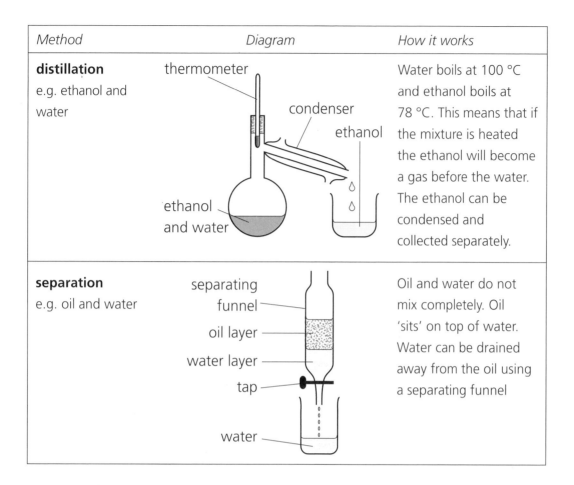	Water boils at 100 °C and ethanol boils at 78 °C. This means that if the mixture is heated the ethanol will become a gas before the water. The ethanol can be condensed and collected separately.
separation e.g. oil and water		Oil and water do not mix completely. Oil 'sits' on top of water. Water can be drained away from the oil using a separating funnel

6.5 Metals and non-metals

Metals are found on the left-hand side of the Periodic Table. Most metals are shiny solids at room temperature and are good thermal and electrical conductors. Only a few metals are magnetic, for example iron.

Non-metals are found on the 9 _____ -hand side of the Periodic Table. Many non-metals are gases at room temperature, for example oxygen, nitrogen and chlorine. Non-metals tend to be poor thermal and electrical conductors.

We can tell if an element is a metal or a non-metal by its physical properties.

Evidence	Metal or non-metal?
a shiny solid, not magnetic, good thermal conductor	metal
good electrical and thermal conductor	metal
dull appearance, poor thermal conductor	non-metal
gas at room temperature, poor electrical conductor	10 _____

Answers can be found on page 38

Changing materials

7.1 Physical changes

When physical changes take place there is no change in mass (it is conserved). Some examples of physical changes are:

● changes of state, e.g. from a solid to a liquid, and
● the formation of solutions, e.g. dissolving sugar in water.

A solid lump of gold has a mass of 10 g. The gold is then heated until it melts and becomes a liquid. The mass of the liquid will be **1**_____ g.

The mass of a sugar solution is 25 g. It was made by completely dissolving some sugar in 20 g of water. The mass of sugar used was **2**_____ g.

A **solution** is made when a **solute** dissolves in a **solvent**. Different solutes have different solubilities (the amount of solute which dissolves) in different solvents. An increase in temperature often increases the solubility of a solute.

Different materials have different melting points and boiling points – they **change state** at different temperatures.

● Water has a melting point of 0 °C and a boiling point of **3**_____ °C.
● Ammonia has a melting point of –77 °C and a boiling point of –33 °C.
● Iron has a melting point of 1537 °C and a boiling point of 2927 °C.

This means that at room temperature (25 °C), water will be a liquid, ammonia a gas and iron a **4**_____. But on a very cold day when the temperature is –5 °C, water will be a solid (ice).

When a substance changes state there is a transfer of energy. To make a solid melt it needs to be heated. By heating the solid you are supplying the particles of the solid with energy – enough to allow them to move apart and change to the liquid state. If the heat source is then removed the liquid will start to cool down and change back to a solid. The liquid transfers its thermal (heat) energy to its surroundings.

	energy supplied		energy supplied	
SOLID	⟶	LIQUID	⟶	GAS
	⟵		⟵	
	energy released		energy released	

Answers can be found on page 38

As more energy is supplied, by increasing temperature, the particles move around more. This requires more space and so the material will **5**_____ (get bigger). As the temperature decreases the particles move around more slowly and the material will contract (get smaller).

7.2 Geological changes

Rocks are made from crystals or grains of minerals. Changes in the climate cause rocks to **weather** (erode).

When rocks are heated by the sun they expand and when rocks cool down they **6**_____. The large forces caused by expansion and contraction cause rocks to break down into smaller pieces.

In cold weather, any water that has collected in the cracks in the rock will freeze. When water turns to ice it expands. This causes the cracks to widen and the forces break down the rocks into smaller pieces.

There are three main groups of rock: **sedimentary**, **igneous** and **metamorphic**. They can be linked together by the rock cycle.

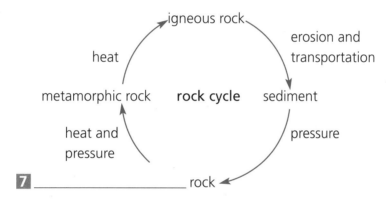

The type of rock and the minerals in the rock depend on how it was formed.

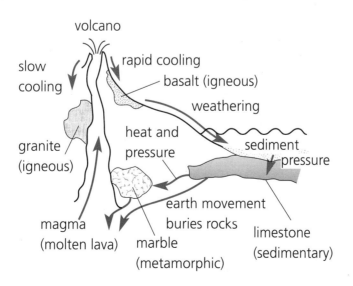

Answers can be found on page 38

23

7.3 Chemical reactions

When a chemical reaction takes place, the total mass of the **reactants** (starting materials) will equal the total mass of the **products** (plus any left-over reactants).

- 12 g carbon + 32 g oxygen will make 44 g carbon dioxide.
- 14 g carbon + 32 g oxygen will make 44 g carbon dioxide and 2 g of carbon will be left over.

Nearly all materials are made by chemical reactions. Sodium and chlorine react together to make sodium chloride. A word equation can be written to show this reaction:

sodium + $\boxed{8}$_____ ⟶ sodium chloride

There are very many different types of reaction, including oxidation and reduction.

In **oxidation** reactions oxygen is added or hydrogen is taken away.

magnesium + oxygen ⟶ magnesium oxide   (magnesium is oxidized)

hydrogen sulphide + oxygen ⟶ sulphur + water
                                          (hydrogen sulphide is oxidized)

Reduction reactions often involve the removing of oxygen or the addition of hydrogen. They are the opposite of oxidation reactions.

Thermal decomposition is when chemicals break down into simpler chemicals when they are heated.

calcium carbonate $\xrightarrow{\text{heat}}$ calcium oxide + carbon dioxide

Chemical reactions are used to make useful products: iron is made from iron oxide, aluminium from aluminium oxide, and zinc from zinc oxide.

The **corrosion** of metals is an example of a chemical reaction that is not useful. Corrosion occurs when a metal reacts with oxygen and water in the air. Corrosion of iron is called rusting. Rusting can be prevented by stopping iron from reacting with either oxygen or $\boxed{9}$_____ or both. Methods of preventing rusting include oiling, greasing, painting or coating the iron with zinc (galvanizing) or with plastic.

Combustion occurs when a substance (usually a fuel) burns in oxygen and gives off energy. The energy could be used for heating (as in a gas fire) or producing electricity (as in a power station).

Unfortunately some of the fossil fuels such as coal and oil contain sulphur. When the fuel is burnt it gives off sulphur dioxide which combines with water in the air to give $\boxed{10}$_____ rain. Acid rain is a pollutant.

Answers can be found on page 38

Patterns of behaviour

8.1 Metals

We will look at the following **reactivity series** of metals:

potassium	sodium	magnesium	aluminium	zinc	iron	lead	copper	gold

*most
reactive*   *least
reactive*

The reactions of metals are summarized in the following table:

	Reaction of the metal with		
	oxygen	*water*	*acids*
potassium	reacts without heating to form metal oxide	reacts rapidly with cold water to form hydrogen and metal hydroxide	reacts explosively to form hydrogen and the metal salt of the acid
sodium			
magnesium	burns in air to form metal oxide	reacts with ▮1▮_____ (but not cold water) to give oxide and hydrogen	reacts more slowly going down the reactivity series to form hydrogen and the metal salt of the acid
aluminium			
zinc			
iron	forms metal oxide layer on surface when heated in air or oxygen	reacts reversibly to give oxide and ▮2▮_____	
lead		does not react under any conditions	
copper	does not react with oxygen		does not react with dilute acids
gold			

You should be able to predict the position of a metal in the reactivity series from its reactions, and the reactions of a metal from its position in the reactivity series.

Answers can be found on page 38

For example, silver does not react with water, acids or oxygen. Silver must therefore lie at the bottom of the series between the metals copper and **3** _____ .

Manganese lies between aluminium and zinc in the reactivity series. Manganese will react with steam to form manganese oxide and **4** _____ , and will react with dilute hydrochloric acid to form manganese chloride and hydrogen.

More reactive metals displace less reactive metals from aqueous solutions of their salts. The following table summarizes the reactions of zinc, iron and copper with solutions of their corresponding salts.

	zinc sulphate	iron sulphate	copper sulphate
zinc		iron deposited, solution changes from green to colourless	copper deposited, solution changes from blue to colourless
iron	no reaction		copper deposited, solution changes from blue to **5** _____
copper	no reaction	**6** _____	

When copper is added to silver nitrate, **7** _____ will be deposited and the solution will change from colourless to blue.

8.2 Acids and bases

The acidity of a solution can be measured by its **pH**. Litmus, methyl orange and phenolphthalein are examples of pH indicators. They can be used to determine whether a solution is acidic, alkaline or **8** _____ .

Indicator	Colour in		
	neutral (pH = 7)	acids (pH < 7)	alkalis (pH > 7)
Litmus	mauve	red	blue
Methyl orange	orange	red	yellow
Phenolphthalein	colourless	colourless	red

Answers can be found on page 38

Universal indicator (UI) is a mixture of indicators. The colour change at various pHs is that of the visible spectrum.

pH	1	2	3	4	5	6	7	8	9	10	11	12	13	14
colour	red				orange	green	green	blue	dark blue	violet				

A **base** is metal oxide or hydroxide. Magnesium oxide, copper oxide, iron oxide, zinc hydroxide, calcium hydroxide and sodium hydroxide are examples of bases.

Alkalis are bases that dissolve in water. The commonest alkalis are sodium hydroxide, potassium hydroxide and calcium hydroxide.

Note All alkalis are bases, but all bases are *not* alkalis.

Some of the reactions of acids and bases are:

acid + **9** _____ ⟶ salt + hydrogen

acid + base ⟶ salt + water

acid + metal carbonate ⟶ metal salt + **10** _____
                                                                      + water

Indigestion is caused by too much acid in the stomach. Antacids such as sodium hydrogencarbonate, calcium carbonate or magnesium hydroxide are taken to neutralize the acid.

Sometimes soil is too acidic for crops to grow and a base such as lime (calcium oxide) is added to neutralize the soil.

Sometimes the atmosphere contains acidic polluting gases such as sulphur dioxide and nitrogen dioxide. These gases dissolve in water to form acid rain which can corrode metals and chemically weather (erode) rocks.

Answers can be found on page 38

Electricity and magnetism

9.1 Static charge

An **insulator** does not allow an electric current to pass through it. Plastic, rubber, ceramics and air are examples of insulators.

A metal allows an electric current to pass through it. All metals are

1 _____.

Insulators can be charged by friction, e.g. by rubbing a balloon on your jumper. The static charge created may be positive or negative.

● Like charges repel one another.
● Unlike charges **2** _____ one another.

9.2 Current in circuits

A battery provides a voltage to push electrons round a circuit, creating an electric current. An ammeter is used to measure **3** _____.

We use different symbols to represent components when we draw circuit diagrams.

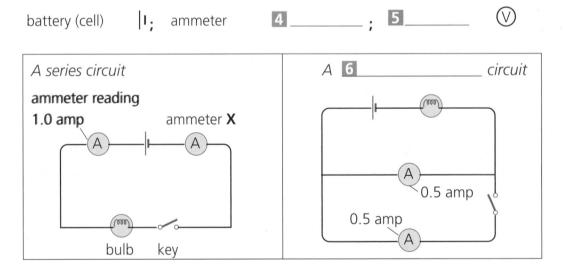

battery (cell) |I; ammeter **4** _____ ; **5** _____ Ⓥ

Current is *not* 'used up' by the various components in a circuit. The current that leaves the battery is the same as the current returning to the battery. The current in ammeter **X** is **7** _____.

The current in a circuit can be increased by increasing the number of cells in the circuit. The current will decrease if more bulbs are added to the circuit or if the number of cells is decreased.

Answers can be found on page 38

9.3 Magnetic fields

A magnet has a magnetic field around it. The pattern of magnetic field lines produced by a bar magnet is shown.

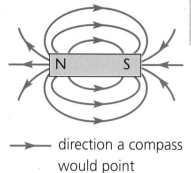

Magnets attract iron and **8**_____ (an alloy of iron) but they do not attract many other metals such as copper, magnesium or zinc.

→ direction a compass would point

9.4 Electromagnets

A magnetic field is formed when an electric current passes through a coil (see a)). You can remember which end is the north pole by placing the fingers of your right hand in the direction in which the current flows round the coil. Your thumb will point to the north pole (see (b)).

Electromagnets are made by wrapping a coil of wire around an **9**_____ core (see (c)).

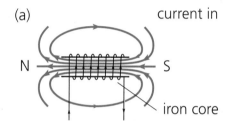

(a)   current in

N — S

iron core

(b)

current direction

N

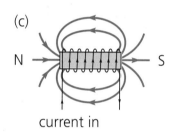

(c)

N — S

current in

Electric bells and relays use electromagnets.

In the electric bell circuit when the switch is on, the armature is attracted to the **10**_____ and the striker hits the bell. However, the circuit is broken at the adjustable screw when this happens, and the striker springs back. Contact is re-made and the process is repeated. The bell will continue to ring as long as the switch is on.

An electric bell circuit

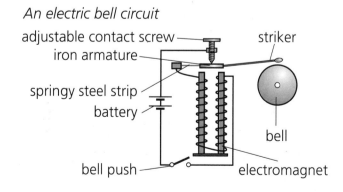

adjustable contact screw — striker
iron armature —
springy steel strip —
battery —
bell
bell push — electromagnet

A relay circuit

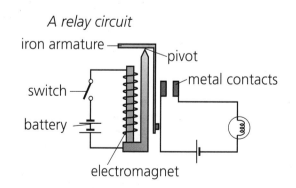

iron armature —
pivot
metal contacts
switch —
battery —
electromagnet

In the relay circuit you should be able to work out why the light goes on when the switch in the relay is on.

Answers can be found on page 38

Forces and motion

10.1 Force and linear motion

To work out the **speed** of an object you need to know the distance it travels and the time it takes.

$$\text{speed} = \frac{\boxed{1}\rule{4cm}{0.4pt}}{\text{time}}$$

The speed of a car can be measured in miles per hour.

If the forces on a moving object are not balanced the object will speed up or slow down. A stationary object will not move because the forces on the object are balanced.

Friction is a force that tries to prevent $\boxed{2}$_____. Friction can sometimes be an advantage and sometimes it can be a disadvantage. Friction between a car tyre and the road is vital for the car to move and for it to $\boxed{3}$_____ down without skidding.

The more tread there is on a tyre the greater the friction. There are very strict rules about how much tread there should be on a tyre. If there is too little, it would be difficult to stop the car quickly.

A parachutist slows down because of the $\boxed{4}$_____ resistance.

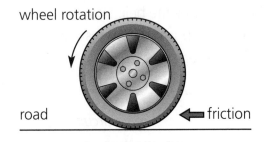

10.2 Force and rotation

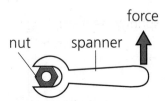

The point about which things turn round is called the $\boxed{5}$_____. You may have used a spanner to undo a nut. You only have to apply a small force to the handle of the spanner to make the nut turn.

Answers can be found on page 38

The pivot on each of the following is shown by the letter P.

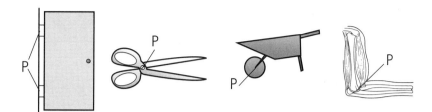

The turning effect of a force is called the **moment** of the force. It depends upon the size of the force and the ⑥_____ from the force to the fulcrum (pivot).

moment of force = size of force × distance of the force from the fulcrum

Look at the see-saw shown here.

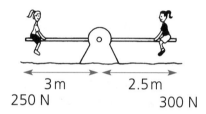

3 m   2.5 m
250 N   300 N

When the see-saw is level the forces are ⑦_____.

 clockwise moments = anti-clockwise ⑧_____

250 newtons × 3 metres = 300 newtons × 2.5 metres

10.3 Force and pressure

pressure $= \dfrac{\text{force}}{\text{area}}$

If you weigh 300 newtons (N) and the total area of the soles of your feet is 0.25 m² then the pressure you exert on the ground will be $\frac{300}{0.25}$ = 1200 N per m². But, if you put on snow shoes with a total area of 1.5 m² then the pressure you would exert on the ground would be ⑨_____ N per m². People wear snow shoes to stop them sinking into the snow.

The reason why sharp blades on a knife cut you is because the force applied on the blade is large and the surface area of the blade is very ⑩_____ .

Answers can be found on page 38

Light and sound

11.1 The behaviour of light

The diagram shows how a shadow is formed on a surface.

Shadows prove that light travels in **1**_____ lines

Light travels at a finite speed. It travels much faster than sound.

Non-luminous (dark) surfaces scatter light. This light enters our eyes so that we can **2**_____ the object.

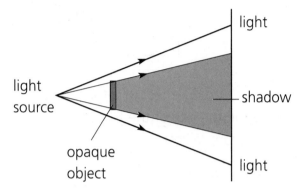

Smooth surfaces such as mirrors **reflect** **3**_____ .

When light passes from air through a glass block it is **refracted**. Refraction occurs at the boundaries between air and glass.

When white light is passed through a glass prism it may be **dispersed** (separated out) to give a range of colours. These are the colours you see in a rainbow.

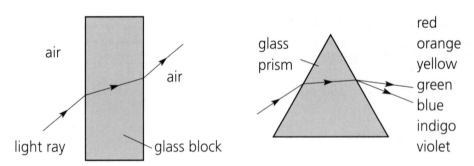

The **primary** colours are blue, red and **4**_____
The **secondary** colours are cyan, magenta and yellow.

A primary colour filter only lets through its own colour, e.g. a blue filter only lets through **5**_____ light. Secondary filters let through the primary colours that make the secondary colour of the filter, e.g. a magenta filter lets through red light and **6**_____ light.

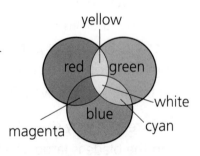

Paints and dyes reflect light. A red jumper looks red in white light because it absorbs all the colours except red which it reflects. A yellow jumper in white light reflects **7**_____ and green. A yellow jumper would look green in cyan light and black in blue light.

Answers can be found on page 38

11.2 Hearing

Sound waves cause our ear drums to vibrate. We all have different ranges of sound that we can hear. As we get older, it is more difficult to hear sounds with a high pitch.

Loud sounds such as explosions can **8**_____ the ear drum.

11.3 Vibration and sound

Sound waves cannot travel through a **9**_____ .

The loudness of a sound depends upon the **amplitude** of the vibration causing the sound. The louder the sound, the larger the amplitude.

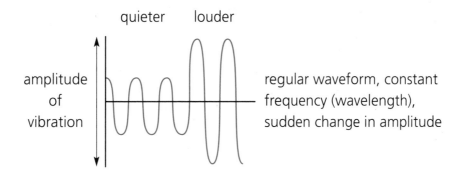

The pitch of a note depends upon the **frequency** of the vibration. The higher the frequency, the higher the **10**_____ of the note.

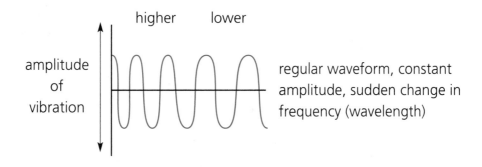

Answers can be found on page 38

33

The Earth and beyond

The Universe has everything in it – matter, energy and space. The biggest 'building blocks' in the Universe are **galaxies**. Each galaxy is made up of many millions of **1**_____. Our Sun is one of the stars in one of the many millions of galaxies. The **2**_____ is at the centre of our **solar system**.

There are five main types of objects in the solar system. They are:

Objects	Properties
stars	give out heat and light, e.g. the Sun
planets	orbit the Sun; reflect the light of the Sun, e.g. Earth
3_____	orbit planets; reflect the light of the Sun
asteroids	orbit the Sun and reflect its light; sometimes called planetoids (small planets)
comets	have huge orbits around the Sun; made up of rocky ice; recognisable by their 'tail' of dust and vapour; reflect the light of the Sun

Day and night, and the changes in the position of stars in the night sky, occur because the Earth spins on its axis. As the Earth rotates, different countries are in sunlight.

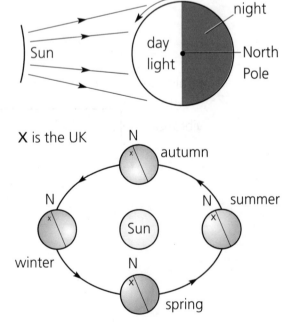

The seasons can be explained by the fact that the Earth's axis is tilted as shown in the diagram. For a place **X** on the Earth, when the North Pole points towards the Sun it is summer, and when the North Pole points away from the Sun it is winter.

Answers can be found on page 38

The order of the planets from the Sun can be remembered by using this sentence:

Mary's **V**iolet **E**yes **M**ake **J**ohn's **S**taying **U**p **N**ights **P**leasant

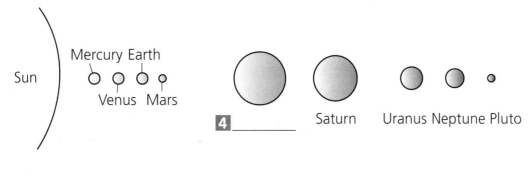

Mercury Earth

Sun

Venus Mars

4_____

Saturn   Uranus Neptune Pluto

Gravity is the 5_____ between two or more objects. In the solar system the size of the gravitational force on a planet depends upon:

- the mass of the planet, and
- how far it is from the Sun and from other planets in the system.

The orbital motion of planets in the solar system is due to the gravitational forces acting between the Sun and the 6_____ .

The Sun and other stars give out light and heat. The Sun appears very bright to us because it is so much nearer than other stars. It is the only star that can be seen during the daytime. Energy from the Sun supports all life on 7_____ . The planets and the Moon 8_____ light received from the Sun.

Artificial satellites are used to observe the Earth, to provide communication links and to explore the solar system. The Hubble Space Telescope is a satellite that is used to observe space.

Communication satellites are put into geostationary 9_____ . These satellites stay in the same position relative to the 10_____ .

Answers can be found on page 38

Energy resources and energy transfer

13.1 Energy resources

There are many different forms of energy, including chemical, electrical, thermal (heat), kinetic, light, potential and sound. This makes it is very difficult to say what energy really is. We use energy to make things work. Anything that causes movement has energy.

There are a great variety of energy resources including oil, gas, coal, biomass, wind, waves and batteries. The ultimate source of most of the Earth's energy resources is the **1**_____. Coal was formed from giant **2**_____ that lived many millions of years ago. When coal is burnt you could say that you are getting the stored energy from all those years ago. Coal is sometimes called 'bottled sunshine'.

Energy cannot be created or **3**_____. It can be converted from one form of energy to another form of energy.

Electrical energy is generated using a variety of resources. Coal, oil, gas or biomass can be burnt to heat water to produce steam. The high pressure steam turns a turbine which then turns a generator to produce **4**_____.

The **fossil fuels** oil, gas and coal are examples of **non-renewable** energy resources because they cannot be made in our lifetime. Plants, such as trees, are **5**_____ energy resources; they can be replaced over and over again.

There are other renewable sources of energy that we can use.

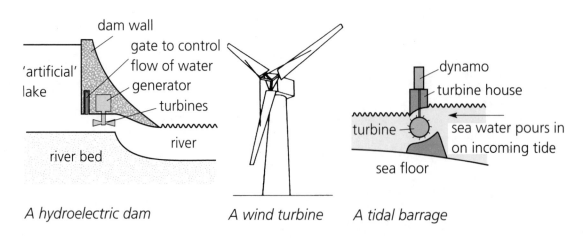

A hydroelectric dam   *A wind turbine*   *A tidal barrage*

Answers can be found on page 38

Hydroelectric power uses the potential energy of **6**_____ stored behind dams.

Wind turbines (windmills) use the kinetic energy of the **7**_____ to turn generators.

Tidal power uses the potential energy of the tides to turn generators. Tides are caused by the relative movement of the Moon and the Earth.

Waves, which have both potential energy (energy of position) and **8**_____ energy (energy of movement), can be used to turn generators.

Geothermal energy and solar energy can be used to heat water.

The heat from the Sun plays an important part in the **water cycle**. Water evaporates from ground level and is deposited as rain to form reservoirs in the hills and mountains.

13.2 Conservation of energy

Temperature measures how hot something is. There are two main scales for measuring temperature: Celsius (°C) and Fahrenheit (°F). The temperature of a normal healthy person is 37 °C or 98.4 °F.

The heat energy that something has depends upon several factors, including temperature and mass. For example, 100 grams of water at 30 °C has ten times more energy than 10 grams of water at 30 °C, although both are at the same temperature.

Energy cannot be created or destroyed but it can be converted from one form to another, transferred from place to place, and **9**_____. One convenient way of storing energy is in a battery. The chemical energy stored in the battery is converted to electrical energy when it is used.

All the energy we use eventually ends up as **10**_____ energy. It is very difficult to get this energy back.

For almost any source of energy it should be possible for you to trace its origin back to the Sun. For example, think of an electric fire.

energy from Sun ➤ chemical energy in coal ➤ heat energy from burning coal ➤ kinetic energy of turbine ➤ electrical energy ➤ heat energy in element of electric fire

Answers can be found on page 38

Answers to self-check questions

For some questions other answers might be acceptable – check with your teacher or your text book.

Topic 1 Life processes and cell activity
1 brain
2 liver
3 kidneys
4 heart
5 roots
6 stem
7 organs
8 chloroplasts
9 cell wall
10 cytoplasm

Topic 2 Humans as organisms
1 proteins
2 fats
3 enzymes
4 anus
5 veins
6 skeleton
7 testes
8 ovaries
9 oxygen
10 drugs

Topic 3 Green plants as organisms
1 photosynthesis
2 oxygen
3 root (hairs)
4 petal
5 sepal
6 stigma
7 fruit
8 water
9 aerobic
10 carbon dioxide

Topic 4 Variation, classification and inheritance
1 discontinuous
2 environment
3 genes
4 snail
5 robin
6 squirrel
7 groups
8 animals
9 invertebrates
10 birds

Topic 5 Living things in their environment
1 habitat
2 environment
3 plants
4 omnivores
5 consumers
6 producers
7 consumers
8 prey
9 resources
10 natural selection

Topic 6 Classifying materials
1 no
2 yes
3 yes
4 gas
5 O
6 potassium
7 oxygen O_2
8 water
9 right
10 non-metal

Topic 7 Changing materials
1 10 g
2 5 g
3 100
4 solid
5 expand
6 contract
7 sedimentary
8 chlorine
9 water
10 acid

Topic 8 Patterns of behaviour
1 steam
2 hydrogen
3 gold
4 hydrogen
5 green
6 no reaction
7 silver
8 neutral
9 metal
10 carbon dioxide

Topic 9 Electricity and magnetism
1 conductors
2 attract
3 current
4 Ⓐ
5 voltmeter
6 parallel
7 1.0 amps
8 steel
9 iron
10 electromagnet

Topic 10 Forces and motion
1 distance
2 movement
3 slow
4 air
5 pivot
6 distance
7 balanced
8 moments
9 $\frac{300}{1.5} = 200$
10 small

Topic 11 Light and sound
1 straight
2 see
3 light
4 green
5 blue
6 blue
7 red
8 damage
9 vacuum
10 pitch

Topic 12 The Earth and beyond
1 stars
2 Sun
3 moons
4 Jupiter
5 force
6 planets
7 Earth
8 reflect
9 orbits
10 Earth

Topic 13 Energy resources and energy transfer
1 Sun
2 plants
3 destroyed
4 electricity
5 renewable
6 water
7 wind
8 kinetic
9 stored
10 heat

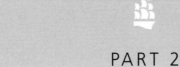

PART 2

Test practice papers

After working through Part 1, try each of the practice papers.

Taking the practice tests

- Find a place at home where you are comfortable and where it is reasonably quiet.
- Make sure you have a pencil, ruler and a calculator.
- You could set an alarm clock to go off after 60 minutes. But if you haven't finished, carry on until you have.

By timing yourself in this way, you will become more aware of just how much time you will have in the National Test itself.

Marking the questions

You will find the answers and a detailed breakdown of the marks awarded on pages 65–75.

The first part of each test has questions at Levels 5 and 6. The last six questions in Test 1 and the last two questions in Test 2 are at Level 7. The Level of each question is indicated in the answers.

Instructions

- Each test is 1 hour long.
- You will need a pen, a pencil, a ruler and a calculator.
- Look out for the command words used in the questions, such as 'Give' and 'Suggest'. A list and their meanings is given on page 40.
- Try to answer *all* the questions. If you find a question too hard, go on to the next question.
- The lines and spaces give you a clue as to the length of answer required. Also look at the mark awarded for each section of a question. If there are 2 marks then two separate points are required.
- Write all your answers in the book. Do not use any rough paper.
- Check your work carefully.
- Ask your teacher or parent if you are not sure what to do.

Once you have attempted the tests, ask your parent to mark your answers.

Now, read through these command words and their explanation, then try the following tests.

Words commonly used in examination questions

Calculate (work out)

The question involves maths. You should show your working.

Example

Q A girl is standing on one leg. Her weight is 180 N. The pressure on her shoe is 1.50 N/cm². Calculate the area of her shoe.

A Pressure $= \dfrac{weight}{area}$ so area $= \dfrac{weight}{pressure}$

area $= \dfrac{180}{1.5} = 120 \text{ cm}^2$

Describe

You should write down what you do, or what you would see, in as much detail as possible.

Example

Q Describe the changes in energy of a ball when you throw it up and catch it again.

A Kinetic energy changes into potential energy as the ball goes up; potential energy changes into kinetic energy as it comes down.

Explain

You should give a reason for your answer.

Example

Q Explain how feathers insulate a bird in cold weather.

A Feathers trap air, and air is a poor conductor of heat.

Give/state/write down

You should write down the answer.

Example

Q Give two ways in which humans differ from trees.

A Humans can move from place to place; trees are stationary.

Humans use up oxygen; trees use up carbon dioxide.

Suggest

You have to use your knowledge of science and the information in the question to give what you think is the best answer.

Example

Q Suggest why oceanic plates sink underneath continental plates.

A Because the oceanic plate is denser than the continental plate.

Test 1

Q1 Using only the words

   fruit leaf ovary root seed stem vein

identify **A**, **B**, **C** and **D** on the diagram of the dandelion.

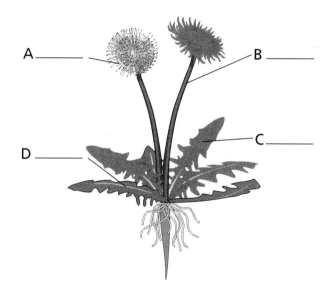

A_____

B_____

C_____

D_____

4
Q1

maximum 4 marks

Q2 Look at the following food web.

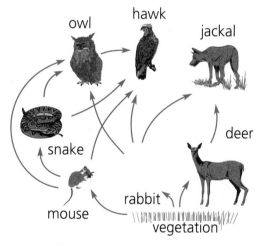

Identify each of the following:

i the producer

....

1
Q2 i

ii the herbivores

....

1
Q2 ii

Answers can be found on page 65

iii the small carnivores

Q2 iii

1

iv the large (top) carnivores.

Q2 iv

1

maximum 4 marks

Q3 **a** One of the functions of fruit is to help spread seeds. Seeds can be spread in a number of ways. Draw lines to match each fruit with its means of spreading.

Fruit	Means of spreading
cherry	fruit eaten by birds
goose grass	fruit explodes and scatters the seeds
poppy	fruit floats through the air
sycamore	fruit sticks to clothes and animals

4

Q3 a

b In humans the seeds are sperm cells.

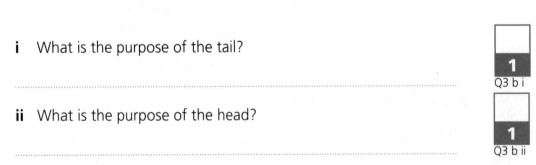

head

tail   nucleus

i What is the purpose of the tail?

1

Q3 b i

ii What is the purpose of the head?

1

Q3 b ii

maximum 6 marks

Answers can be found on page 65

Q4 Your teacher has made the apparatus below to demonstrate breathing.

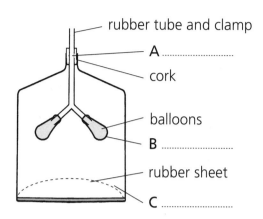

rubber tube and clamp

A ....

cork

balloons

B ....

rubber sheet

C ....

Next to each label, **A**, **B** and **C**, write the equivalent part of the human system.

3

Q4

maximum 3 marks

Q5 The following flow diagram can be used to find out if a compound is soluble or insoluble in water.

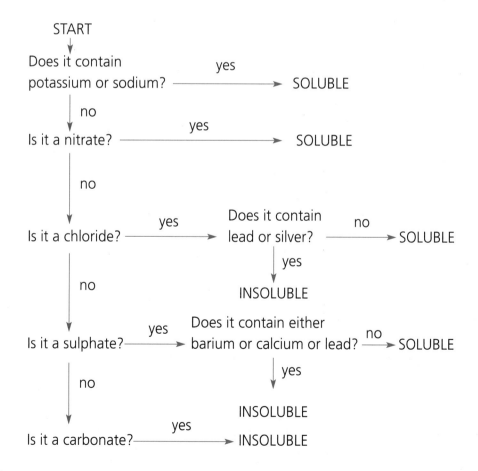

START

Does it contain potassium or sodium? — yes → SOLUBLE

no

Is it a nitrate? — yes → SOLUBLE

no

Is it a chloride? — yes → Does it contain lead or silver? — no → SOLUBLE

yes

INSOLUBLE

no

Is it a sulphate? — yes → Does it contain either barium or calcium or lead? — no → SOLUBLE

yes

INSOLUBLE

no

Is it a carbonate? — yes → INSOLUBLE

Answers can be found on page 66

State whether each of the following compounds is soluble or insoluble.

a i Potassium nitrate ....

ii Silver chloride ....

b Describe briefly how you would obtain lead sulphate from a mixture of zinc sulphate and lead sulphate.

....

....

maximum 5 marks

Q6 The table below gives a list of liquids together with their melting points and boiling points.

Liquid	Melting point °C	Boiling point °C
A	0.0	100.0
B	−39.0	357.0
C	−117.0	78.5
D	16.6	118.0

a Which liquid would you use in a thermometer to measure:

i both the melting point and the boiling point of water? ....

ii the temperature of a warm oven (250 °C)? ....

iii a temperature in the Antarctic of −60 °C? ....

b Which liquid would turn to a solid on a cold day (10 °C)? ....

Answers can be found on page 66

c Suggest why liquid **C** has a red dye added to it when this liquid is used in a thermometer.

....

....

1
Q6 c

maximum 5 marks

Q7 You decide to try and stop your friend from smoking. You set up the following apparatus.

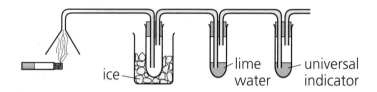

Water is collected in the first tube; the lime-water in the second tube gave a white precipitate and the universal indicator in the third tube turns red because sulphur dioxide has dissolved in the water.

a Name **three** elements that must be present in a cigarette.

.... , ... and ....

3
Q7 a

b Explain why some carbon monoxide is formed when a cigarette burns.

....

....

1
Q7 b

maximum 4 marks

Q8 This question is about changes in state.

Fill in the gaps **A**, **B**, **C** and **D**.

Change of state	Common name	Energy given out or taken in
gas to liquid	condensation	given out
liquid to solid	**A**	given out
B	melting	taken in
C	evaporating	**D** ....

4
Q8

maximum 4 marks

Answers can be found on pages 66 and 67

Q9　**a**　Complete the ray diagram below (using a ruler and pencil) to show the position of the image of the bulb in the mirror.

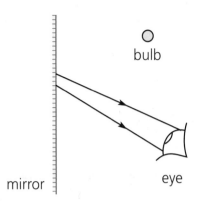

mirror

bulb

eye

2

Q9 a

b　The above arrangement could be used in an experiment to prove that:

the angle of .... equals the angle of

....

2

Q9 b

maximum 4 marks

Q10　The diagram below shows a model of a Pulsating Water Engine (PWE). Before the candle is lit the copper pipe is filled with water. As soon as the water starts to boil, steam is forced out of the pipe and the boat moves across the water.

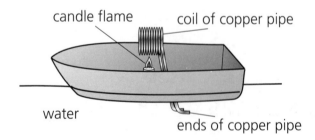

candle flame　　coil of copper pipe

water

ends of copper pipe

a　Fill in the gap to show the energy changes that take place.

chemical energy
(from candle) ⟶ .... ⟶ kinetic energy

1

Q10 a

b　Suggest why copper pipe is used and not magnesium pipe.

1

Q10 b

....

Answers can be found on page 67

c Only 35% of the chemical energy is converted into kinetic energy. Explain what happens to the 'lost' energy.

....

....

2

Q10 c

d Explain why, after the steam has condensed, water goes back into the pipe.

....

1

Q10 d

maximum 5 marks

Q11 You are given:

two identical bulbs   one battery   two identical ammeters

Draw circuit diagrams to show:

a a series circuit, placing the ammeters so that they have the same reading

2

Q11 a

b a parallel circuit , placing the ammeters so that they have different readings.

2

Q11 b

maximum 4 marks

Q12 Complete the following sentences by using only words from the list below.

Earth   Galaxy   Jupiter   Mercury   moon   orbit   satellite   star

a The Sun is a .... found in the Milky Way. The nearest planet to the Sun is .... An artificial .... can be used to view the Earth from space.

3

Q12 a

Answers can be found on pages 67 and 68

The table below gives some information about four planets. Use this information to answer the following questions.

Planet	Density (kg/m³)	Period of orbit (one 'year')	Time to rotate on axis (one 'day')
Earth	5.5	$365\frac{1}{4}$ days	24 hours
Jupiter	1.4	11.9 years	9.9 hours
Saturn	0.7	29.5 years	10.66 hours
Venus	5.3	225 days	243 days

b Which planet has a longer 'day' than 'year'?

....

1
Q12 b

c Suggest a reason why the density of Saturn is so low.

....

1
Q12 c

maximum 5 marks

Q13 The diagram shows the bones in the upper and lower leg.

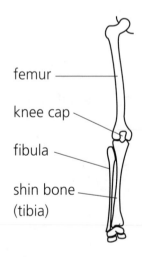

femur

knee cap

fibula

shin bone
(tibia)

a Beside it, show the bones in the lower and upper arm in a similar way.

3
Q13 a

b Give **two** uses of the skeleton

....

....

2
Q13 b

maximum 5 marks

Answers can be found on pages 68 and 69

Q14 The diagram shows a small branch of a tree. Photosynthesis takes place in the green leaves on the branch.

a Complete the word equation to show what happens during photosynthesis:

water + ... + energy from sunlight

⟶ .... + oxygen

2
Q14 a

b Name the green pigment present in leaves.

....

1
Q14 b

c What is the role of this pigment in photosynthesis?

....

1
Q14 c

d Suggest why it is an advantage for plants to have large leaves.

....

1
Q14 d

maximum 5 marks

Q15 The chart below shows the percentage (%) of six materials that have been replaced by plastics.

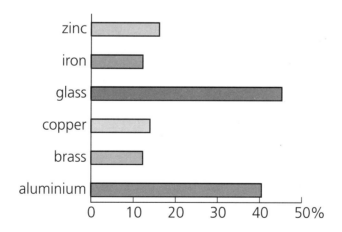

a Which of these materials has been replaced the most by plastics?

....

1
Q15 a

b Give **one** example where plastic has replaced iron.

....

1
Q15 b

c Why are most door knockers made of brass and not plastic?

....

1
Q15 c

Answers can be found on page 69

d Suggest why cooking foil is made of aluminium and not plastic.

....

1
Q15 d

e Give **one** use of copper that will never be replaced by plastic.

....

1
Q15 e

maximum 5 marks

Q16 Mercury is a silver coloured liquid. It is a metal.

a How would you show that mercury was a metal?

....

1
Q16 a

A red powder is formed when mercury is heated in air for a long time. The red powder is mercury oxide.

b Would the mercury oxide weigh more or less than the mercury from which it was made? Explain your answer.

....

....

1
Q16 b

Magnesium is more reactive than mercury.

c What would you **see** if you added magnesium metal to a solution of mercury nitrate?

....

....

2
Q16 c

maximum 4 marks

Q17 The toy shown in the diagram was made using common materials.

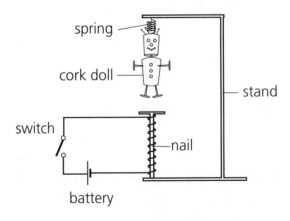

Answers can be found on pages 69 and 70

a When the switch is closed the doll moves downwards. Explain in detail how this happens.

....

....

....

2
Q17 a

b When the switch is released the doll moves upwards. Explain in detail how this happens.

....

....

2
Q17 b

maximum 4 marks

Q18 The diagram below shows a simple weighing machine.

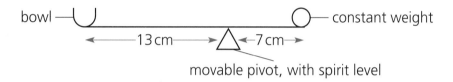

bowl — constant weight
←—13 cm—→ ←7 cm→
movable pivot, with spirit level

The weight of the bowl is 35 g and the constant weight on the right-hand side is 65 g. The pivot can move left and right. It balances when it is 13 cm from the bowl and 7 cm from the constant weight. The pivot point has a spirit level.

Complete the table below.

Distance from pivot to 65 g weight (cm)	Distance from pivot to bowl (cm)	Mass in bowl (g)	Total mass of bowl + contents (g)
7.0	13.0	0.0	35.0
10.0	10.0	**A** _____	65.0
B _____	8.0	62.5	97.5
C _____	**D** _____	160.0	195.0

4
Q18

maximum 4 marks

Answers can be found on page 70

Test 2

Q1 The following changes occur at puberty. Put these changes in three lists: boys only; girls only; and both boys and girls.

breasts develop   menstruation starts
emotional changes   penis gets larger
facial hair grows   pubic hair grows

Boys only	Girls only	Both boys and girls

4
Q1

maximum 4 marks

Q2 The drawing below shows some of the main features of a plant cell.

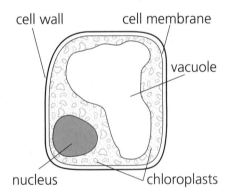

cell wall   cell membrane

vacuole

nucleus   chloroplasts

Draw lines to join each of the named components with its function. The first one has been done for you.

Component   *Function*

cell membrane   stores useful substances

cell wall   makes food by photosynthesis

chloroplasts   controls the movement of substances
                       into and out of the cell

nucleus   maintains the shape of the cell

vacuole   makes protein

3
Q2

Answers can be found on page 71   *maximum 3 marks*

Q3 Animals can be classified as vertebrates and invertebrates.

a What are invertebrates?

1

Q3 a

....

b Invertebrates can be classified into the following six phyla:
anthropods, platyhelminthes, annelids, nematodes, echinoderms
and molluscs, using the following key.

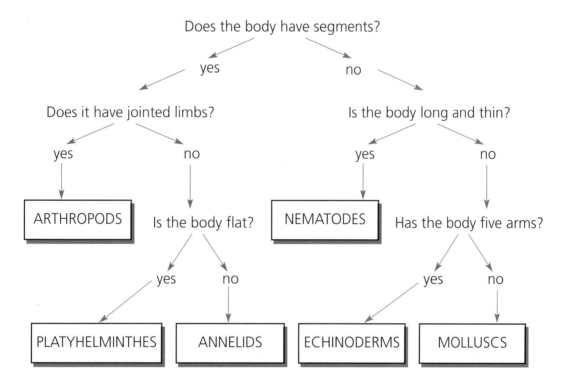

Does the body have segments?

yes — Does it have jointed limbs?

no — Is the body long and thin?

Does it have jointed limbs?
yes → ARTHROPODS
no → Is the body flat?

Is the body long and thin?
yes → NEMATODES
no → Has the body five arms?

Is the body flat?
yes → PLATYHELMINTHES
no → ANNELIDS

Has the body five arms?
yes → ECHINODERMS
no → MOLLUSCS

Classify each of the following into the six groups using the above key.

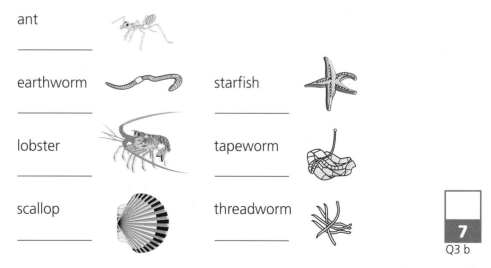

ant
_____

earthworm
_____

starfish
_____

lobster
_____

tapeworm
_____

scallop
_____

threadworm
_____

7

Q3 b

maximum 8 marks

Answers can be found on pages 71 and 72

Q4 Mixtures can be separated by a variety of methods. The diagrams below give five different ways of separating liquids.

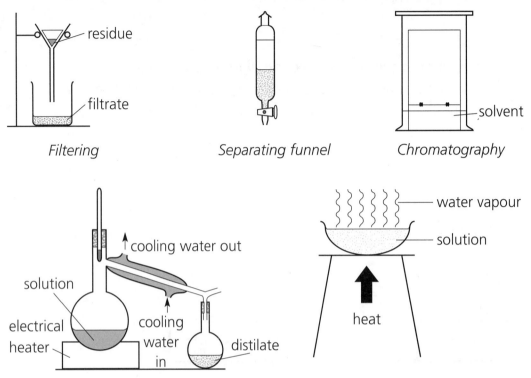

Filtering   Separating funnel   Chromatography

Simple distillation   Evaporation

Which method would you use to separate each of the following?

a sodium chloride from a solution of sodium chloride and water

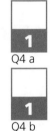

Q4 a

b water from inks dissolved in water

Q4 b

c oil from a mixture of oil and water

Q4 c

maximum 3 marks

Q5 Indicators change colour at different pHs. The table opposite shows the colour of various indicators at different pHs.

a Water has a pH of 7. What will be the colour of methyl orange in water?

Q5 a

Answers can be found on page 72

pH	1	2	3	4	5	6	7	8	9	10	11
congo red	blue		mauve		red						
litmus	red				mauve			blue			
methyl orange	red		orange		yellow						
phenol-phthalein	colourless								red		
thymol blue	red	yellow						green		blue	

Sodium carbonate solution has a pH of 8 and sodium hydrogen carbonate solution has a pH of 11.

b Which indicator would you use to distinguish between these two solutions?

....

Q5 b

Chromatography was used to analyse a mixture of indicators. The results shown below were produced when water (pH 7) was used as the solvent:

mixture   methyl orange   phenol–phthalein   litmus   thymol blue   congo red

yellow ☐
blue ☐
mauve ☐
red ☐

Answers can be found on page 72

When the paper was held over fumes of ammonia (pH10) the chromatogram changed colour:

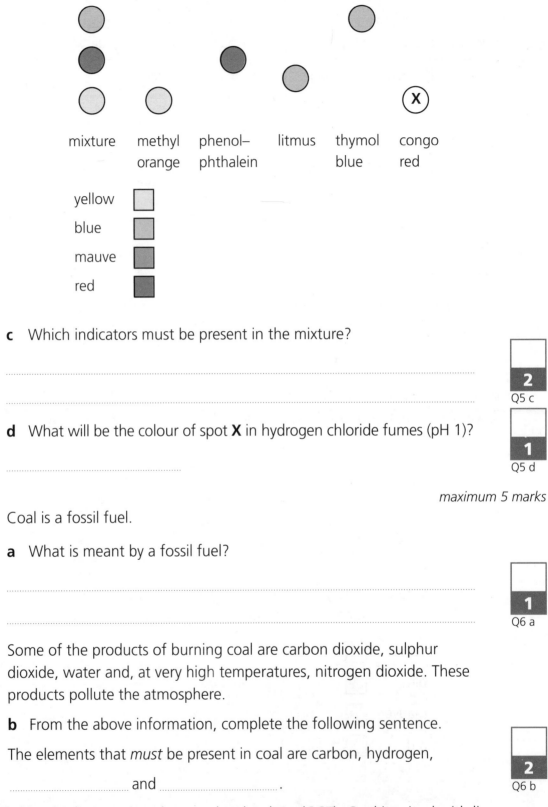

| | mixture | methyl orange | phenol-phthalein | litmus | thymol blue | congo red |

yellow ▢

blue ▨

mauve ▨

red ▧

c Which indicators must be present in the mixture?

....

....

2
Q5 c

d What will be the colour of spot **X** in hydrogen chloride fumes (pH 1)?

....

1
Q5 d

maximum 5 marks

Q6 Coal is a fossil fuel.

a What is meant by a fossil fuel?

....

....

1
Q6 a

Some of the products of burning coal are carbon dioxide, sulphur dioxide, water and, at very high temperatures, nitrogen dioxide. These products pollute the atmosphere.

b From the above information, complete the following sentence.

The elements that *must* be present in coal are carbon, hydrogen,

.... and ....

2
Q6 b

Coal is now burnt using clean coal technology (CCT). Coal is mixed with lime (calcium oxide) and burnt, at a low temperature, over a cushion of air.

Answers can be found on page 72 and 73

c Suggest two reasons why this method of burning coal reduces the pollutants entering the atmosphere by about 90%.

....

....

....

....

1
2

Q6 c

maximum 5 marks

Q7

Metal	Colour of metal	Colour of solution of compound in water	Description of reaction
copper	brown	copper sulphate solution is blue	when silver is added to copper sulphate there is no reaction; when iron is added to copper sulphate the solution turns green and a brown solid is formed
iron	dark grey	iron sulphate solution is green	when copper is added to iron sulphate there is no reaction; when silver is added to iron sulphate there is no reaction
silver	white	silver nitrate is colourless	

a Using the above information, put the elements copper, iron and silver in the order of their reactivity. Put the most reactive metal first.

1
1

Q7 a

....

(most reactive)   (least reactive)

b Describe what you would see if you added copper to silver nitrate solution.

....

....

1
2

Q7 b

maximum 3 marks

Answers can be found on page 73

Q8 Wood is an important energy resource.

a The energy stored in wood came from the Sun. Describe how the energy from the Sun became stored in the wood.

....

....

| 1 |
Q8 a

b Explain why wood is a renewable source of energy.

....

....

| 1 |
Q8 b

c Name two non-renewable sources of energy.

....

....

| 2 |
Q8 c

d In France the River Rance is used to generate electricity using the machinery shown simplified in the diagram.

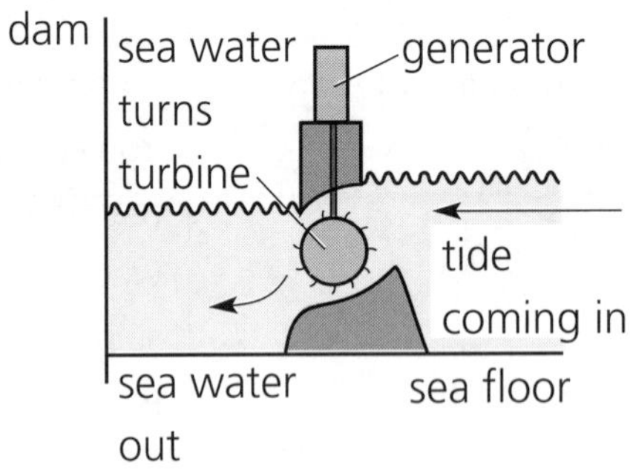

dam | sea water
turns
turbine
sea water
out

generator

tide
coming in
sea floor

Explain how electricity is generated.

....

....

....

| 3 |
Q8 d

During breaks in sporting events such as football and tennis, large numbers of people switch on their kettles to boil water to make a pot of tea. One way of overcoming this problem of the large demand for electricity is to use the type of power station shown below. Water is pumped into the artificial lake at night, when electricity is cheap.

Answers can be found on page 73

Water is released at peak times to produce energy.

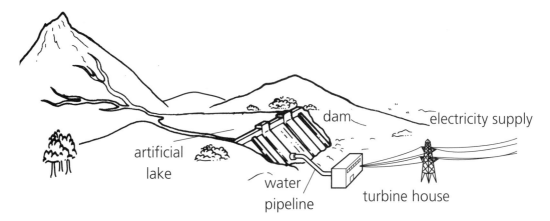

e What name is given to this method of producing electricity?

1
Q8 e

....

maximum 8 marks

Q9 The graph below shows how far a motorist travels in given intervals of time.

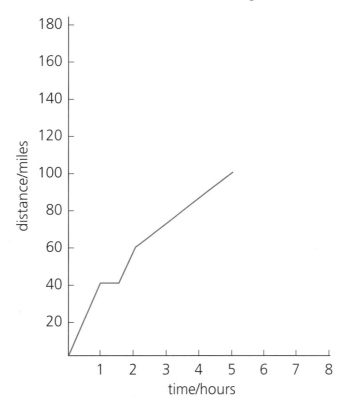

a How far does the motorist travel in the first hour?

1
Q9 a

....

b For how long did the motorist stop for petrol?

1
Q9 b

....

Answers can be found on pages 73 and 74

c What is the motorist's average speed for the first 2 hours of his journey?

....

`1`
Q9 c

The motorist stops for lunch 5 hours after leaving home. The total time spent over lunch was 1 hour. He then continues his journey at the same speed as your answer to **c** and he reaches his destination after a further 2 hours.

d Complete the graph above to show his whole journey.

`2`
Q9 d

maximum 5 marks

Q10 A brass drawing pin is shown in the diagram below.

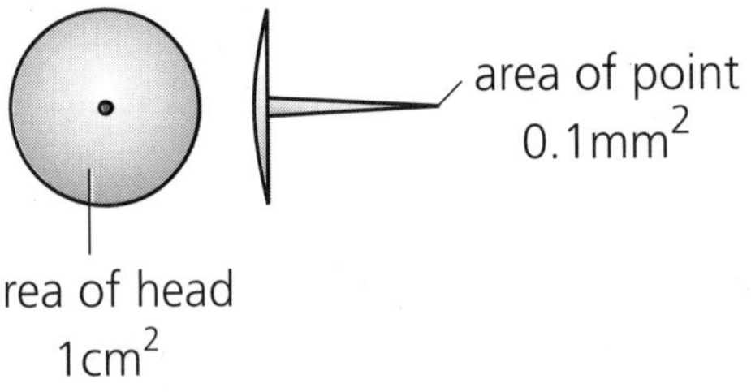

area of point
0.1mm^2

area of head
1cm^2

a Why is it easier to push the pointed end into cardboard than the head of the pin? (Tick the correct answer).

There is less pressure because a large
surface area is in contact with the cardboard. ☐

There is less pressure because a small
surface area is in contact with the cardboard. ☐

There is more pressure because a large
surface area is in contact with the cardboard. ☐

There is more pressure because a small
surface area is in contact with the cardboard. ☐

`1`
Q10 a

b If the pin was attached to a mass of 60 N, what would be the pressure exerted by the head of the pin on the board? Give the units.

....

....

`2`
Q10 b

maximum 3 marks

Answers can be found on pages 73 and 74

Q11 Males and females have different sex chromosomes. Males have an X and a Y. Females have two Xs.

a Which one of the following statements is TRUE?

    A The X chromosome is bigger than the Y chromosome.

    B The Y chromosome is bigger than the X chromosome.

    C The X chromosome and the Y chromosome are the same size.

    The TRUE statement is ....

Q11 a

b Which of the following are present in chromosomes? Place a ✓ against those present.

    bacteria ☐

    DNA ☐

    protein ☐

    virus ☐

    water ☐

Q11 b

A disease commonly known as 'nastione' can be inherited. An X chromosome carrying 'nastione' is shown as **X**. In order for a person to develop the symptoms of 'nastione' two **X** chromosomes are required.

Both parents are carriers of 'nastione'; that is the mother is **X**X and the father is **X**Y.

c Complete the table below to show:

Chromosome combinations	Male or female	Symptoms/carrier /free of disease
XY	male	carrier
XX	A _____	B _____
C _____	female	D _____
E _____	F _____	free of disease

Q11 c

d What are the chances of a couple who are both carriers of 'nastione' having a child who is *not* a carrier of 'nastione'? Circle the correct answer.

    1 in 1   1 in 2   1 in 3   1 in 4

Q11 d

maximum 7 marks

Answers can be found on page 74

Q12 Rocks are divided according to their origin into *sedimentary*, *metamorphic* and *igneous rock*.

The diagram below shows part of the rock cycle.

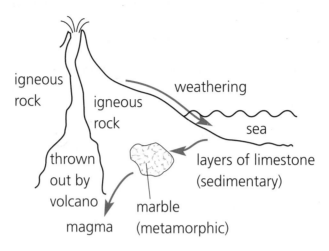

a What igneous rock is formed when magma cools

i quickly? ....

1
Q12 a i

ii slowly? ....

1
Q12 a ii

b Suggest why marble (a type of metamorphic rock) is formed in the position shown.

....

1
Q12 b

c Rocks are broken down by weathering. There are three main types of weathering: *mechanical*, *chemical* and *biological*.
   i One example of physical weathering is when rocks are heated to a high temperature and then cooled. Give another example of physical weathering.

....

....

1
Q12 c i

   ii Chemical weathering is brought about by rain water reacting with rocks such as limestone. Name the gas that dissolves in water to form carbonic acid.

....

....

. **1**
Q12 c ii

Answers can be found on pages 74 and 75

iii Biological weathering occurs when plants grow in rocks. Explain how the roots of plants cause rocks to weather.

....

....

1
Q12 c iii

d Explain why sedimentary rock often contain fossils.

....

....

....

1
Q12 d

Tectonic activity can cause rocks of all types to become buried deep underground.

e What is meant by tectonic activity?

....

1
Q12 e

Q13 Look at the following four sound waves. *maximum 8 marks*

| A | B | C | D |

a Which waves have

i the same wavelength? .... and ....

1
Q13 a i

ii the same amplitude? .... and ....

1
Q13 a ii

b Which of the sounds is

i the loudest? ....

1
Q13 b i

ii the lowest pitch? ....

1
Q13 b ii

Answers can be found on page 75

The following three wave patterns were formed by a piano, a tuning fork and a violin.

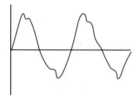 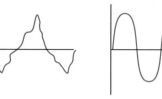

E   F   G

c Which sound, **E**, **F** or **G**, was produced by the tuning fork? Explain your answer.

....

Q13 c

d How can you tell that the same note was being played in each case?

....

Q13 d

A note on a piano has a frequency of 220 cycles per second (hertz) and a wavelength of 1.5 metres in air. Sound travels ten times faster in steel than in air.

e In steel,
  i what is the frequency of the note?

....

Q13 e i

  ii what is the wavelength of the note?

....

Q13 e ii

maximum 8 marks

Answers can be found on page 75

Answers: Test 1

An asterisk (*) indicates that 1 mark is awarded for this answer. The topic number given tells you the topic in Part 1 of this book on which the question is based.

Q1 LEVEL 5/TOPIC 1

A seed*   **B** stem*   **C** leaf*   **D** vein*

`4`

tip *Questions on the parts of plants and their functions are very common.*

Q2 LEVEL 5/TOPIC 5.2

i   vegetation*
ii mice, rabbit (and deer)* (allow mark for mice and rabbit)
iii snake, owl (and hawk)* (allow mark for snake and owl)
iv hawk and jackal*

`4`

tip *Green plants such as grass are the producers. Herbivores eat green plants. Carnivores eat animals. Human beings eat plants and animals; we are omnivores.*

Q3 LEVEL 6/TOPIC 3.2

a   cherry ———————— fruit eaten by birds

goose grass   fruit explodes and scatters the seed

poppy   fruit floats through the air

sycamore   fruit sticks to clothes and animals

(1 mark for each correct line; but if you have drawn more than one line from the same fruit, award no marks for that part)

`4`

b i   To make the sperm move (along the egg tubes)*
            (Allow any word that means move, e.g. swim)
ii To break through the membrane of the egg (and fertilize it)*
            (Allow any word that implies that the sperm enters the egg)

tip *The dispersal of seeds is very important. It helps the new plants to grow because they will have more light, food and water. Make sure you understand the difference between sexual reproduction in plants and asexual reproduction in plants.*

`2`

Q4 LEVEL 6/TOPIC 2.5

A trachea*   **B** lung*   **C** diaphragm*

`3`

tip *'Breathing' describes the mechanical process of air entering and leaving the lungs; respiration is the chemical reaction that takes place to form carbon dioxide, water and energy.*

Q5 LEVEL 5/TOPIC 6.4

a i   soluble*

   ii   insoluble*

`2`

b   Add excess water*; heat and/or stir*; filter*

   (Allow centrifuge but *no* other method is acceptable)

`3`

tip *Solubility is very important. Nitrates are very soluble in water. If farmers add too much fertilizer containing nitrates to their soil it will dissolve in rain water and eventually end up in our rivers, causing environmental problems.*

Q6 LEVEL 5/TOPIC 7.1

a i   **B***

   ii   **B***

   iii   **C***

`3`

b D*

`1`

c   Liquid C is colourless; the dye makes it visible*

   For your information:

   A is water;   B is mercury;   C is ethanol;   D is ethanoic acid

`1`

tip *If the melting point and boiling point of a substance are below room temperature (about 20 °C), it will be a gas; if they are both above room temperature, the substance will be a solid. However, if the melting point is below room temperature and the boiling point is above room temperature then the substance will be a liquid.*

Q7 LEVEL 6/TOPIC 7.3

a   Carbon*, hydrogen*, sulphur*

   (*Do not allow* oxygen)

b   Incomplete combustion* (or words to that effect)

`3`

`1`

tip *Hydrogen in water; carbon from carbon dioxide, and sulphur from sulphur dioxide. The oxygen could have come from the air.*

tip *Any carbon-containing compound that burns in a limited supply of oxygen will produce the lethal gas carbon monoxide. This is why rooms containing a gas burner must be well ventilated.*

Q8 LEVEL 6/TOPIC 6.1

    A freezing* (Allow solidification)

    B solid to liquid*

    C liquid to gas*

    D taken in*　　　　**4**

> **tip** *Evaporation (liquid to gas) takes place at temperatures below the boiling point of the liquid. Liquids with low boiling points are said to be volatile.*

Q9 LEVEL 5/TOPIC 11.1

a

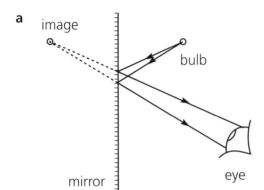

    Lines must be straight*; image must be as far behind the mirror as the object is in front of the mirror*　　　　**2**

b incidence*, reflection* (Can be in either order)　　　　**2**

> **tip** *In a plane mirror, the image is always formed as far behind the mirror as the object is in front. The image is also laterally inverted, i.e. your right eye looks like your left eye in the mirror. This is because light travels in straight lines.*

Q10 LEVEL 5/TOPIC 13.1

    a heat energy* (or thermal energy)　　　　**1**

    b Copper does not react with steam* (or magnesium reacts with steam)　　　　**1**

    c Converted into light energy*, sound energy*, heat energy*
       (Any two; can be in any order; accept thermal energy for heat energy)　　　　**2**

    d A vacuum is formed and water rushes in to fill the vacuum*
       (Do not allow siphoning)　　　　**1**

> **tip** *Energy cannot be created or destroyed. It is converted into other forms of energy.*

Q11 LEVEL 6/TOPIC 9.2

a

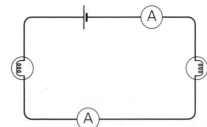

Must be a series circuit*; all components must be included*
(Components can be in any order)

2

b

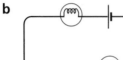

Must be a parallel circuit*; the ammeters must be in the correct positions*
(Check to make sure that the ammeters would have different readings)

2

tip *In a series circuit the order of the components does not matter.*

Q12 LEVEL 6/TOPIC 12

a star*, Mercury*, satellite*
(Must be in correct order; do not allow 'moon' for 'satellite')

3

b Venus*

1

c It is made up mainly of gases*
(Allow named gases, such as ammonia or hydrogen)

1

tip *The order of the planets from the Sun can be remembered by the mnemonic or saying:*

Mary's Violet Eyes Make John's Staying Up Nights Pleasant

(Mercury, Venus, Earth, Mars, Jupiter, Saturn, Uranus, Neptune and Pluto)

Q13 LEVEL 7/TOPIC 2.3

a

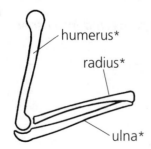

humerus*

radius*

ulna*

3

b Gives shape*; gives support*; produces blood cells*; protects internal organs*; allows movement*
(Any two)

`2`

tip *Bones are hard, dense substances but they are hollow in the middle. The hollow is filled with bone marrow. Red blood cells are formed in the marrow.*

The rib cage protects the lungs and the heart.

Q14 LEVEL 7/TOPIC 3.1

    a carbon dioxide*; glucose*
      (Must be on correct sides of the equation; allow carbohydrate for glucose but *not* starch)

`2`

    b chlorophyll*

`1`

    c Absorbs energy (from sunlight)*

`1`

    d So that they can absorb more sunlight*

`1`

$$6 CO_2 + 6 H_2O + energy = C_6H_{12}O_6$$

tip *Photosynthesis is the opposite of respiration. In respiration.*
glucose + oxygen → carbon dioxide + water.

Q15 LEVEL 7/TOPIC 6.5

    a glass*

`1`

    b water containers* (Allow buckets, bowls)

`1`

    c Plastic does not give a 'metallic' ring*

`1`

    d Plastic would melt, or plastic does not conduct heat*
      (Allow plastic would catch fire)

`1`

    e As a conductor of electricity*
      (Allow electric wiring; do not allow pots and pans)

`1`

tip *Many items that used to made of metals or alloys are now made of plastics. Plastics are less dense and do not rust.*

Q16 LEVEL 7/TOPIC 8.1

    a See if it conducts electricity*
      (Allow no other answer)

`1`

tip *All metals conduct electricity.*

b More, because it has reacted with oxygen from the air (and hence the weight will increase)*
(No mark for 'more' by itself)

`1`

c a silver coloured* liquid* (is formed)
(Allow 1 mark if you say that mercury is formed)

`2`

> **tip** *More reactive metals displace less reactive metals from their compounds. Note, the question asked what would you **see**, not what is formed.*

Q17 LEVEL 7/TOPIC 9.4

a The current flowing in the coil causes the nail to become an electromagnet*; the iron legs of the doll are attracted to the electromagnet*
(You need to mention the fact that the legs of the doll must be made of iron)

`2`

b There is no current so the nail loses its magnetism*; the stretched spring pulls the cork doll upwards*

`2`

> **tip** *Electromagnets lose their magnetism as soon as the current is turned off. Bar magnets keep their magnetism, unless they are hammered or heated.*

Q18 LEVEL 7/TOPIC 10.2

A 30.0g*
B 12.0 cm*
C 15.0 cm*
D 5.0 cm*
(Answers to 1 decimal place. There is no need to put in the units)

`4`

> **tip** *Clockwise moments = anti-clockwise moments*

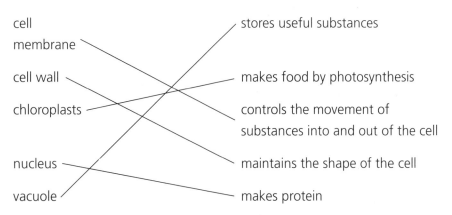

Test 2

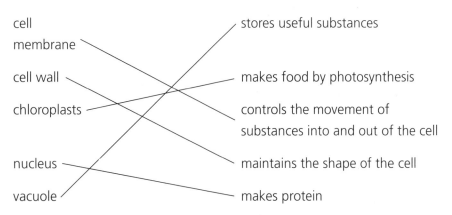

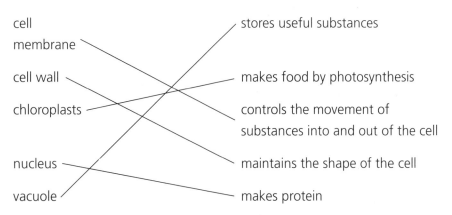

 ANSWERS

Q1 LEVEL 5/TOPIC 1

Boys only
Facial hair grows; penis gets larger*
(Both have to be stated to get 1 mark)

Girls only
Menstruation starts; breasts develop*
(Both have to be stated to get 1 mark)

Both boys and girls
Pubic hair grows*; emotional changes*

4

> **tip** *Puberty is when a boy or a girl starts growing into a man or a woman respectively. It usually starts at about the age of 11 or 12 years. Other changes that take place in boys include the larynx enlarging, the voice deepening and body muscles developing. Changes for girls include the uterus and vagina getting larger and the hip girdle widening.*

Q2 LEVEL 5/TOPIC 1

cell membrane ⟶ stores useful substances

cell wall

chloroplasts ⟶ makes food by photosynthesis

nucleus ⟶ controls the movement of substances into and out of the cell

vacuole ⟶ maintains the shape of the cell

⟶ makes protein

3

(4 correct lines – 3 marks; 3 correct lines – 2 marks; 2 correct lines – 1 mark; if you have drawn more than one line from the same component, award no marks for that part)

> **tip** *Make sure you know the similarities and differences between plant cells and animal cells. Both plant cells and animal cells have a nucleus and cell membrane.*

Q3 LEVEL 6/TOPIC 4.2

a Animals that do not have backbones*

1

b ant – arthropod*
earthworm – annelid*
lobster – arthropod*
scallop – mollusc*
starfish – echinoderm*
tapeworm – platyhelminthes*
threadworm – nematode*

`7`

tip *Animals with backbones are called vertebrates.*

Q4 LEVEL 5/TOPIC 6.4

a evaporation*

`1`

b simple distillation*

`1`

c separating funnel*

`1`

(Only the apparatus shown can be used; do not accept other methods such as fractional distillation)

tip *Make sure you know when to use each method. If you want a solid from a solution, you must use evaporation; if you want the liquid (solvent) from a solution, you must use distillation.*

Q5 LEVEL 5/TOPIC 8.2

a yellow*

`1`

b phenolphthalein*

`1`

c thymol blue, phenolphthalein, methyl orange
(3 correct – 2 marks; 2 correct – 1 mark)

`2`

d blue

`1`

tip *Note thymol blue has several colour changes. Universal indicator has been developed to give the colours of the rainbow:*

red	orange	yellow	green	blue	indigo	violet
4	5	6	7	8	9	10

Q6 LEVEL 6/TOPIC 7.3

a Fuel formed from the decaying remains of (marine) animals and/or plants which lived millions of years ago*
(You must mention decaying animals or plants)

`1`

b sulphur*, nitrogen* (No marks for oxygen) `2`

c Temperature not high enough to form nitrogen dioxide*; calcium oxide
reacts and removes the acid gases*
(Allow either carbon dioxide or nitrogen dioxide for acid gases removed by
the lime) `2`

> **tip** *All fossil fuels burn to form carbon dioxide and water. In a limited
> supply of air, carbon monoxide is formed which is highly poisonous.
> Always make sure that there is plenty of air available when burning
> fuels. The oxygen in the compound comes from the air – although coal
> may contain this element the oxygen in the products does not
> necessarily come from the coal.*

Q7 LEVEL 6/TOPIC 8.1

a iron, copper, silver* (Must be in correct order – no mark if order is reversed) `1`

b White solid is formed*; solution turns blue*
(Allow silver-coloured solid) `2`

> **tip** *More reactive metals always displace a less reactive metal
> from a solution. Thus iron would displace silver from silver nitrate
> solution, but silver would not displace copper from copper
> sulphate solution.*

Q8 LEVEL 5/TOPICS 13.1, 13.2

a Energy is required for photosynthesis – this energy comes from the Sun*
(You must mention photosynthesis) `1`

b It can be produced in a short timescale*
(You must refer to timescale) `1`

c coal*; oil*; gas*
(Any two) `2`

d Tide ebbs and flows*; incoming water turns turbine*;
turbine turns generator*
(Allow 'goes out and comes in' for 'ebbs and flows') `3`

e hydroelectricity* (Allow just 'hydro') `1`

> **tip** *Non-renewable energy sources took a long time to form. All
> energy can be traced back to energy obtained from the Sun. All
> energy eventually ends up as heat energy.*
>
> *We are always looking for new ways to make electrical energy.*

Q9 LEVEL 6/TOPIC 10.1

   a 40 miles* (Units must be stated)   `1`

   b 30 minutes* (or $\frac{1}{2}$ hour)   `1`

   c 30 miles per hour* (Units must be stated)   `1`

   d Graph horizontal for 1 hour after 5 hours*; slope correct for the next 2 hours*   `2`
      (The graph should end at 160 miles after 8 hours)

> **tip** *Average speed = total distance travelled/total time taken. In this case 60 miles/2 hours, so the average speed was 30 miles per hour. When he stops, the graph is horizontal. The slope of the graph gives the speed.*

Q10 LEVEL 6/TOPIC 10.3

   a There is more pressure because a small surface area is in contact with the cardboard*   `1`

   b 60* N cm^{-2}* (Accept N/cm^2)   `2`

> **tip** *This was tricky because it asked for the head on the board, not the point! You must take care to read the question. Pressure = force/area – in this case 60/1.*

Q11 LEVEL 6/TOPIC 4.1

   a **C***   `1`

   b DNA*, protein*   `2`
      (Chromosomes contain a small amount of protein)

   c **A** female **B** carrier*
      C XX, **D** symptoms*
      E XY, **F** male*   `3`
      (For each pair you must have both correct to score the mark)

   d 1 in 4*   `1`

> **tip** *Chromosomes usually occur in pairs in most cells. In normal human beings there are 46 chromosomes (23 of each) but Down's Syndrome people have 47 chromosomes.*

Q12 LEVEL 7/TOPIC 7.2

   a **i** pumice*
      (Accept other correct answers such as basalt)
      ii granite*   `2`

   b Rocks have been subjected to high temperature and high pressure*   `1`
      (You must mention both temperature *and* pressure)

c i Water gets inside the cracks in the rocks, the water freezes and expands causing the rock to break up*

(You need to express this general idea of expansion of ice and breaking down of rocks)

ii carbon dioxide* (No other answer is acceptable)

iii roots force themselves into the rocks causing them to break down*

(Or other statement that expresses this idea)

3

d Soil is taken into the sea by rivers and settles on the sea bed where over the years, under heat and pressure, it turns to sedimentary rock, burying marine animals as it does so*

(Or other ways of expressing this general idea)

1

e earth movements*

1

tip *The total amount of rock on the Earth remains constant because of the rock cycle. Sedimentary rock might contain fossils. Rapid cooling of magma produces small crystals e.g. pumice; slow cooling of magma produces granite.*

Q13 LEVEL 7/TOPIC 11.3

a i B and D*
  ii A and B*

2

b i D*
  ii A *

2

c G It produces a single wave pattern*

1

d They all have the same wavelength*

1

e i 220 cycles per second*
  ii 15 metres*

2

tip *The same wavelength means the same note. The same height of the wave means the same degree of loudness. The shorter the wavelength the higher the note (pitch). A tuning fork produces a 'pure' note.*

tip *Wavelength = wave speed/frequency.*
Since the wave speed is 10 times faster and the frequency remains constant, the wavelength in steel must be 10 times longer.

Marking Grid

Test 1 (pages 41–51)

Question	Marks available	Marks scored
1	4	
2	4	
3	6	
4	3	
5	5	
6	5	
7	4	
8	4	
9	4	
10	5	
11	4	
12	5	
13	5	
14	5	
15	5	
16	4	
17	4	
18	4	
total	80	

Test 2 (pages 52–64)

Question	Marks available	Marks scored
1	4	
2	3	
3	8	
4	3	
5	5	
6	5	
7	3	
8	8	
9	5	
10	3	
11	7	
12	8	
13	8	
total	70	

Using the marking grid

	Test 1	Test 2	Test 1+2
Maximum mark	80	70	150
Level 3 or below	up to 24	up to 21	up to 46
Level 4	25–32	22–28	47–60
Level 5	33–42	29–37	61–79
Level 6	43–50	38–43	80–93
Level 7 or above	51–80	44–70	94–150

Mark scored in Test 1 [　　] ▶ Level [　　]

Mark scored in Test 2 [　　] ▶ Level [　　]

Total [　　] ▶ Level [　　]